Edward Stack

Six Months in Persia

Vol. 1

Edward Stack

Six Months in Persia
Vol. 1

ISBN/EAN: 9783337310462

Printed in Europe, USA, Canada, Australia, Japan

Cover: Foto ©Andreas Hilbeck / pixelio.de

More available books at **www.hansebooks.com**

SIX MONTHS IN PERSIA.

BY

EDWARD STACK,
BENGAL CIVIL SERVICE.

IN TWO VOLUMES.
VOL. I.

London:
SAMPSON LOW, MARSTON, SEARLE, & RIVINGTON,
CROWN BUILDINGS, 188, FLEET STREET.
1882.

CONTENTS.

CHAPTER I.
BAREILLY TO BUSHIRE 1

CHAPTER II.
BUSHIRE TO SHIRAZ 29

CHAPTER III.
PERSEPOLIS 55

CHAPTER IV.
SHIRAZ TO FIRUZABAD 71

CHAPTER V.
FIRUZABAD 86

CHAPTER VI.
FIRUZABAD TO LAR 96

CHAPTER VII.
LAR 133

CHAPTER VIII.

Lar to Saidabad. . . . 146

CHAPTER IX.

Saidabad to Karman 183

CHAPTER X.

Karman 198

CHAPTER XI.

Karman to Yazd . . . 221

CHAPTER XII.

Yazd 256

CHAPTER XIII.

Shirkuh 271

SIX MONTHS IN PERSIA.

CHAPTER I.

BAREILLY TO BUSHIRE.

24th January to 13th February.

AFTER eight years in India, I began to be conscious that a change of climate was desirable. On the 24th January, 1881, I left the pleasant station of Bareilly in the North-Western Provinces, intending to embark at Karachi for Bushire, and make my way to Europe across Persia. One Sayyid Ali, a native of Teheran, accompanied me as major-domo, factotum, and travelling-companion. I had known him about five years, he had taught me to speak Persian, and I had lent him occasional assistance in his endeavours to maintain himself in India, a task by no means easy for the hapless foreigner who is stranded in that country without money or a patron.

The Sindh railway having recently been

finished, it was possible to travel with ease and luxury all the way from Lahore to Karachi. Sindh is a province which possesses a strange power of captivating the affections of men condemned to live and work in it for a number of years, but its aspect to the casual visitor is not attractive. So far as can be seen from the railway, the country is one level expanse of white clay, whether bare or covered with tamarisk forest. Few parts of the world can boast of finer dust than is produced here. It is powdered clay, white and impalpable, filling all the air, and imparting a greyish hue to the feathery green branches of the tamarisk, as if they were covered with a dirty kind of hoarfrost. This dust has also remarkable penetrative qualities. It fills the railway-carriages, and follows the traveller into the refreshment-room; he finds it in his soup, in his basin, and on the towel with which he endeavours to clean his face. Next to the dust, the tamarisk-trees of Sindh challenge admiration. They occasionally reach a height of thirty feet, with a girth of eight or nine. Perhaps there is no part of India where this tree flourishes in greater perfection, but in the southern provinces of Persia it attains still larger dimensions.

Travelling through such a country, even by rail, tends to become monotonous; and the break at Rori is gladly welcomed, where low limestone hills run down to the Indus, and the steamer waits to ferry passengers across to Sakkar. Here one may see a quaint picture in blue and grey. On the hither side, the houses of Rori, in a uniform grey tint, rise straight from the water's edge to a height of four and five stories, with rows of windows which look only half oriental, and give the river-face a curious resemblance to the back of some old Scotch town. Sakkar answers from over the river with exactly the same dull colour, while in the middle, on a long island, the walls and huge round bastions of Bakkar cast a grey shade over the blue waters. Her palaces and mosques are built of mud, once made bright with coloured tiles, but these have mostly fallen away. The presence of a newer civilization is proclaimed by the bright red of the brick-built railway station, and of the barracks within the old grey fort; but perhaps our predecessors chose the cooler style of building, and certainly they chose the more picturesque. An air of old-fashioned peacefulness and rest hangs over the whole scene, under the quiet morning light.

Not far from Sakkar is the station of Ruk, where one can change for Afghanistan. The Quetta railway has been carried as far as Nari Gorge, some twelve miles within the Afghan frontier. From Ruk, the line runs to Shikarpur and Jacobabad, through a country which grows barer of trees, till at last all vegetation disappears, and the level desert called *Pat* stretches unbroken for nearly a hundred miles, to the vicinity of Sibi. The Sibi plain produces wheat and rice, watered by the Nari river. As the train draws up to the station, lines of barracks come into view, Government bungalows, storehouses, and other signs of a depôt. Northward and westward, the horizon is fenced round with mountains, whose rocky wall is broken by two main passes—the Bolan, dimly descried to the west, and the Nari Gorge, only seven miles distant to the north. The train runs to the very mouth of the gorge, where a group of small but neatly-finished bungalows marks the farthest point, at present, of the railway which was to have been made to Candahar. Here one has leisure to admire the naked ruggedness of the mountains of Southern Afghanistan. They are of red sandstone, weather-worn into all kinds of fantastic shapes.

Nari Gorge.

During my three days' stay in Nari Gorge, I rode a few miles up the pass. The scenery can scarcely be called grand, but is certainly wild and desolate in the extreme. The pass runs between two mountain-walls which now approach each other and now recede, but always present a succession of sheer precipices, jagged ridges, splintered peaks, cloven ravines, huge slopes of tumbled rocks, and taller mountain-tops in the background grimly overlooking all. Of vegetation, even where water might conceivably lie in ledges or hollows of the shattered hill-sides, there is no trace whatever; all is tawny red stone, glowing under the cloudless heat. This was in January. It is difficult to imagine how work can be carried on in June. The only tolerable feature of the pass is the Nari river. The width of the channel is about 200 yards, but the river fills the whole channel only for a few hours in times of flood. A good macadamized road has been made in the dry bed, by the simple process of removing the larger stones, and covering the remainder with earth and gravel; but as the road goes straight ahead, while the river twists like a snake, there is a ford to be crossed at every mile, with water sometimes knee-deep, sometimes more. In two bends of the stream between Nari station and Kilat-i-Kila (nine miles up the gorge) there languish half a dozen tamarisk bushes, about eighteen inches high and three feet in circumference; these are the vegetable products of this rich river-bottom.

Such is the country which the ex-Candahar railway had just begun to enter when orders came to stop work. The rails, which had already been laid down a mile beyond Nari station, were taken up while I was there, and preparations were being made for the cessation of all work within the gorge. The hewn stones prepared for the culverts were left lying where they had been cut, the coolies were flocking back, and the upper works had already been deserted. It was impossible to witness the change without a feeling of regret for labour bestowed in vain. I believe nearly seventy lakhs (say 550,000l.) had been spent in carrying the railway up the pass, so far as it had gone. Rails had actually been laid for only a mile; but the railway embankment is continuous to Kilat-i-Kila (nine miles), with the exception of one or two small gaps which were to have been filled with culverts, and beyond Kilat-i-Kila work has been done in pieces, extending disconnectedly several miles farther. If an unprofessional critic may hazard an opinion, I should say that the work has been admirably done. The embankment does not, like the road, run through the middle of the gorge, nor cross the stream, but keeps the left bank of the river, close under the eastern mountain-wall, which rises above in sheer cliffs of two hundred and three hundred feet, or slopes suddenly upwards in confused masses of broken crags. In one spot a projecting shoulder of rock has been tunneled through. The roof, however, is less safe than could be wished, for the rock has little hardness and no cohesion. In some places the embankment is thirty feet high. It is built of earth, faced with large round stones from the river, and squared off at the edges with artistic nicety. It winds in graceful curves through the irregular contortions of the pass, at a height safe against floods, except at one point, where the river has been turned to prevent the current from setting against the foot of the embankment. The excellence of the work contrasts strangely with the abominable desolation of the scene around. I was assured that the pass maintains its wild character the whole way to Quetta, and that the scenery up to Kilat-i-Kila is a fair specimen of what may be expected anywhere along the route, save that in the upper portions the road grows somewhat worse, the hills rise higher, and at Spin Tangi (the white narrows) the red rock changes to white, and limestone replaces sandstone. Railways have been carried over more difficult country, and through far grander scenery than that presented by the Nari Gorge route to Quetta, where the hills immediately overlooking the line are only 500 to 800 feet high, and the taller peaks in the background rarely rise to 2000 feet. But had the line been completed as far as Quetta, perhaps no other railway in the world could have matched the sheer savagery, the weird and irreclaimable desolation, of its surroundings. To an ordinary observer, it seems impossible that such a line could ever pay. The worst hill-regions of Persia are hardly so dreary, so hopelessly lifeless, as this arid and trackless mountain-belt, which, with the desert before it and the desert behind it, guards the south-western frontier of our Indian empire.

From Nari Gorge I returned to Ruk, and reached Karachi on the 1st February. Four days later I embarked on board the *Rajputana* steamship of the British India Navigation Company, bound for the Persian Gulf.

6th February.—Before entering the Gulf the traveller enjoys the pleasure of three days' navigation of the Sea of Oman, within sight of the coast of Biluchistan. This seaward province is called Mekran. It presents to the view an unbroken wall of precipitous and pinnacled mountains, varying from 1000 to 3000 feet in height, but always inexpressibly wild and forbidding. They are splintered and cloven and shattered into manifold forms of ruin; it is as if Nature, finding them very bad, had set herself to mar her own handiwork. Seen from an offing of fifteen miles these mountains seem to run down into the sea, but in reality a level strip intervenes between their bases and the coastline. Hour after hour the prospect scarcely changes, while the steamer works her way westwards. It is a more continuous and extensive desolation than that of the Sibi hills, and conveys a stronger impression of an eternity of changeless and dolorous emptiness; "a waste land, where no man comes, or hath come since the making of the world." One might fancy that these savage Mekran hills were peopled with evil spirits. And yet there are two English settlements in this waste and melancholy country. They are the telegraph stations at Ormara and Gwadar, on the inland line which runs along part of the coast of Biluchistan. Ormara is within about sixteen hours' steam of Karachi. A hammer-headed promontory of cliffs projects southwards into the sea, and the village and telegraph station are nestled in the angle between the hammer-head and the shaft. The steamer does not call, and the tiny settlement is not visible from the offing.

7th February, Gwadar.—At Gwadar, however, which is fourteen hours west of Ormara, and quite similarly situated, the *Rajputana* stopped and sent a mail-boat ashore. Gwadar is a village of about 2000 souls, built at the end of a sandy spit, with long cliff-walls stretched out on either hand. The southern wall runs eastward some three miles, and is about 250 feet high; the northern wall rises much higher, and in one part takes the semblance of a cathedral with towers and spires, a mass of white rock quaintly implanted on a platform of yellow sandstone, and measuring perhaps 500 feet in vertical height from its topmost pinnacle to the sea-beach at its feet. Some native craft give an air of life to the bay enclosed by these arms of rock. Gwadar is said to be the coolest station in the Gulf, but its advantages in point of climate can hardly compensate its dreadful loneliness. Moreover, the place has been haunted by fever for some years past. Two telegraph officers and the apothecary were ill with fever when the *Rajputana* called, and the only visible English resident was the superintendent. There is nowhere to go and nothing to do in one's leisure hours. The extreme dirtiness of the village takes away all desire of visiting it a second time. It is governed by a deputy of the Sultan of Muscat, who lives in a tumble-down mud palace, with an old bronze gun at the door—a fine old piece of ordnance, probably of Portuguese manufacture, of great length, and about 32 lbs. calibre.

8th February, Muscat.—From Gwadar the course lies across the Sea of Oman to Muscat on the Arabian coast. Here are mountains of far greater height, and of another form and colour. The general effect is more grand than picturesque, majestic rather than grotesque or horrible. The inland ranges lose their tops in the clouds, and their sides, sloping down in rounded spurs and buttresses, spread into a long table-land above the second range, which again is separated from the sea by a labyrinth of deep valleys and bold rocky peaks. All these mountains are black, and they have the quality of utter bareness in common with the mountains of Mekran. In the far background rise the great dark masses of Jabala Abu Daud (6300 feet), Jabal Tagin (5520 feet), and Jabal Nakhl (7740 feet). Their broad breasts give the eye wide scope to roam over realms of upland, where water and pasture might be expected under the shadow of mountain-tops that seem to rob the clouds of their rain. But the glass tells another tale. These mountains are nought but bare' rock, and the plateau below their summits is a waste land suspended between heaven and earth, a great raised plain all treeless, grassless, covered with fragments of black rock tumbled from the hills. The coast abounds in little coves and bays, which open successively upon the view as the steamer passes by. A few towers, of round or square construction, flying the red flag of the Sultan of Muscat, are perched upon projecting cliffs. But Muscat itself remains invisible, though the white sails of Arab boats proclaim the vicinity of a port. These craft are rigged like an Italian felucca, and recall memories of the Mediterranean. Presently, as the steamer draws nearer to the black rocks, a half-Italian town discloses itself along the margin of a bay. Its tall white houses are marked with a triple row of windows, shaded by green jalousies. This is Matrah; and while one is looking at Matrah, and gradually drawing nearer to it, suddenly Muscat harbour opens on the left hand. First is seen a fort on a headland, then another on a bold point opposite; finally the town comes into view at the bottom of the cove, occupying the whole of the narrow beach, and supported by a picturesque fortress on either hand. The steamer turns to the left, and enters the cove. It is a natural harbour formed by two promontories three quarters of a mile long and 400 feet high. Halfway in, the harbour is narrowed by a spur which juts out from the right-hand or western promontory, and reduces the breadth of the cove from half a mile to one quarter. The left-hand promontory has a battery and round tower at its seaward end, the jutting point is similarly armed, and at the foot of the cove stand two isolated masses of rock on either side of the beach, crowned with battlements and round towers built by

Portuguese hands in the sixteenth century, and little changed since. The space between these two fortresses—a frontage of 300 yards—is filled by the white houses of the town. A wharf with stone steps marks the customs-house, and three houses are conspicuous with flags. The red flag flies over the Sultan's palace, and the Union Jack and Stars and Stripes grace the houses of the British and American Consuls. The Sultan's steam yacht and steam launch lie in the harbour, with a number of native craft, some of which fly the Persian ensign—the two-bladed sword of Ali,[1] white on a red ground. Painted boats are moving about the cove, and crowds of people are bathing or fishing on the beach and along the black rocks under the cliffs. The whole scene is most quaint and picturesque, and the more so for its sudden revelation from the recesses of the lifeless hills. Here is a flourishing city, not without stateliness of its kind, the

---

[1] The royal arms of Persia are the Lion and the Sun, and this is the ensign of the very few Persian craft that ply on the Caspian. But in the waters of the Gulf I saw only this sword of Ali—that *zulfiqar* or *divider*, which is best known to the English reader under its changed name and nature as King Arthur's sword Excalibur.

centre of no small trade, hidden away so cunningly behind the sheltering arms of rock, that one might almost have passed it by unseen. Muscat has been a rare station for pirates in the old days. At present its fortifications are hardly defensible, but they are eminently picturesque. The forts on either side of the town are quaint groups of yellow walls and bastions and circular batteries rising in tiers, perched on the top of black cliffs 100 feet high. A similar collection of old-world fortifications embellishes the extremity of the midway jutting point, while every coign of vantage on the cliff-walls of the cove bears its own battery or martello tower. The armament is various in character and uniform in condition. All the iron guns are rusty, and all the brass guns are green with verdigris. Some of the latter are really fine pieces of ordnance, cast by the Portuguese as far back as 1606 A.D. The iron guns are mostly carronades.

Muscat and its dependencies are governed at present by Sultan Sayyid Turki. His elder brother is the Sultan of Zanzibar. Since the division of empire, the affairs of the younger branch have sadly fallen away. So late as 1864, Muscat harbour owned a 36-gun frigate, several corvettes, brigs, and armed buggalows; but Sayyid Turki has been obliged to sell his frigate to a Parsee firm, and the rest of his fleet seems to have disappeared in the same direction. His government is not wholly secure from civil broils. The principal forts are extensively pitted with cannon-shot, as if they were in the habit of firing at one another; and the mountain country behind the town shelters a half-brother of the Sultan's, who comes down from time to time with his Bedouins, and exacts black-mail. Sayyid Turki's revenues consist of about 110,000 dollars from customs, 30,000 dollars from the British Government, and whatever else he can pick up. He is in embarrassed circumstances, but as he enjoys the advantage of British protection, he need trouble himself but little about his creditors or his enemies. The city which he governs is enclosed on two sides by walls, 700 yards and 250 yards in length respectively, and on two sides by the hills and the sea. The bazaar contains the usual variety of nationalities—long-haired Mekranis, grave Arabs with their girdles stuck full of cutlery, and with matchlock and brass-studded buckler at their backs; Persians in jackets and wide trousers; flat-nosed Africans with brawny

Muscat.

limbs; and the familiar form and features of the mild Hindoo. There are 700 Hindoos under the protection of the British Resident in Muscat. They are traders, and if one may judge by their fat and comfortable appearance, they find the business pay. One does not see many signs of wealth in Muscat bazar. The chief article of wholesale export seems to be dates.[2] But the peculiar product of Muscat is its *halwa*, a confection of wheat-starch, with sugar and almonds, which is at once pleasant and nourishing.

By walking a mile beyond the town, and climbing a low saddle-back which separates the harbour of Muscat from Sudab bay, one can obtain a pretty view of either place. On the one hand lie the town and harbour of Muscat, locked in by the dark, precipitous rocks; on the other, the wide sweep of Sudab bay, with its white sand, blue waters, and green palm-groves. After this, nothing re-

---

[2] Muscat has powerful rivals in this trade. Large quantities of dates are exported from Basrah. A gentleman engaged in the trade recently had the curiosity to inquire where the consignments to England found consumers. He discovered that the date-eaters of these islands live chiefly in the mining districts.

mains to be seen; Muscat is exhausted, and the traveller may return with thankfulness to the pleasant hospitality of the British Resident and the American Consul.

9th February, Jashk.—From Muscat to Jashk is one night's run. Jashk is a telegraph-station of no small importance, being the point whence the cable runs to India, and the land-line to Gwadar and Ormara. It surpasses Gwadar in desolation. The telegraph buildings occupy the end of a long sandy spit, projecting seven miles from a low and dreary coast. Mountains of 5000 feet rise in the background, but they are twenty miles inland, and almost invisible on a hot and hazy day, when all that can be distinctly seen in any direction is sea and sand. As a station, however, Jashk is perhaps the best after Bushire, for the telegraph staff is large, and the charms of ladies' society are not unknown. It used even to support a newspaper, called the *Jashk Howl*, a name sufficiently appropriate to the desert character of the place. Jashk promontory, though Persian territory, is rented by the British Government, and garrisoned by 100 Bombay sepoys. At the extremity of the promontory is an old Mahomedan tomb, noteworthy only as having been mentioned in the earliest chronicles of European travellers in the Gulf.

10th February, Bandar Abbas.—The next port is Bandar Abbas. When Shah Abbas the Great, in unholy alliance with the East India Company, destroyed the classical port of Ormuz, and expelled the Portuguese, he founded Bandar Abbas to perpetuate his victory and his name. There is not much to be said about the town. It stands at the head of a broad and shallow bay, and presents to the sea a long frontage of grey, clay-daubed houses, with numerous badgirs (wind-catchers) or wind-towers rising above their flat roofs. An old stone wall and four ruined towers enclose about one-fourth of the town. The population may amount to 6000 souls. The trade of the place is considerable. It is the port of Karman, Lar, Seistan, and south-eastern Persia generally; the increased security of the roads has of late years encouraged commerce; and the customs' duties, which were worth only 25,000 tomans (about 10,000*l*.) a year in 1871, are rented at 40,000 tomans now, by a Turk of Azarbaijan.

Ormuz island lies on the left hand as the steamer leaves Bandar Abbas. The name of Ormuz has been linked by Milton for ever with the barbaric pearl and gold of the gorgeous East. The only token now remaining of its ancient grandeur is the ruined fort, whose massive walls and bastions stand out against the sky, at the extremity of a low spit of land. The rest of the island is a circular mass of salt, a fantastic arrangement of salt hills confusedly flung together, and remarkable both for form and colour. Three sharp peaks of gleaming white overlook a wilderness of red and purple ridges and cones, at the foot of which, as they sink to the sea, arise strange pyramidal shapes of grey rock or clay. In a space of level ground between the hills and the sea, a few stunted trees mark the site of a palace visited by old voyagers of the sixteenth century, who called the place Tamberlake; but Tamberlake has long disappeared, and its very name is lost. Ormuz, in short, looks more like an enchanted island on the scenes of an extravaganza than a place for human habitation. It would make a wild and wonderful picture, if coloured by the imagination of such a painter as M. Gustave Doré.

As Ormuz is left behind, the steamer passes between Larak on the left and Kishm on the right. Larak is a circular and rocky island, but is not salt. A village and an old Dutch fort of small dimensions stand on the northern shore. The island abounds in conical peaks, one of which is almost mathematically correct from base to summit, like a gigantic model of a cone. Kishm is an island which has some memories for Englishmen. The alliance between Shah Abbas and the East India Company was directed against Kishm as well as Ormuz, and one of the few Englishmen killed in the siege of the small Portuguese fortress which guards the north-eastern extremity of the island was William Baffin, the discoverer of Baffin's Bay, who came from Arctic seas and "regions of thick-ribbed ice," to find a grave under the fierce sun of the Persian Gulf. In 1820, and again in 1850, Kishm was made the rendezvous of a British expeditionary force.

11*th February, Linga.*—From Bandar Abbas to Linga is about sixteen hours' run. The two towns resemble each other in size, situation, and appearance, but Linga has a background of palm-groves, which is wanting to Bandar Abbas. As a port, Linga is of minor importance, the customs being farmed for only 10,000 tomans; but it is a great place for shipbuilding, and deserves honourable mention as having turned out the largest buggalow

(Arab felucca) afloat—the *Dunya* or *World*, of 800 tons burthen. She belongs to an Arab merchant of Bombay, and was employed as a transport ship when the Indian troops were sent to Malta in 1878. She carried the horses of a Bengal cavalry regiment. While the *Rajputana* was lying in Linga roads, we saw a buggalow of 500 tons on the stocks ready for launching, and another of 300 tons was under the hands of the riggers. Some seven miles to the east of Linga, a cluster of palms shelters the village of Kung, once a port of the Dutch, who have left a ruined fort and the shattered walls of a factory as memorials of their occupation. The customs-house of Linga itself is an old Dutch factory. But these relics of European settlements are surpassed in antiquity by the ruins of a fortress on a low flat-topped hill immediately behind Linga. Nobody knows anything about these ruins, except that they date from time immemorial. Such faint and forgotten traces of past greatness are quite in keeping with the general tone of the shores of the Gulf. The aspect of the whole country suggests the idea of natural powers exhausted ages since, and a civilization that ran its appointed course a thousand years ago.

12th February, Bahrein.—Leaving Linga, the steamer crosses again to the Arabian coast. The islands of Bahrein are the most uninteresting places in the Gulf, at least in winter, when the pearl fishery is not going on. Low islands covered with palm-groves, and defended by a couple of square forts with round towers at the corners; two towns built mostly of mud; a crowd of native craft; and a Turkish gunboat decorated with flags in honour of Friday; such was the picture presented by Bahrein. The visitor to Bahrein is supposed to go and see the spring which irrigates the principal island. It rises about three miles from the shore. The way thither runs through date-groves and vegetable gardens, and past the ruins of a city, with a mosque and two minarets still standing. The minarets are in a shaky state, and cannot last much longer; but it is not improbable that before they fall they will be measured, sketched, and described by a competent English officer, who will be able also to make excavations on the site. As for the spring, it is a natural pool of circular form, 20 yards in diameter, and about 20 feet in depth; the water is crystal clear, but slightly brackish.

13th February, Bushire.—On the 13th of

February, after a week's voyage, the *Rajputana* came into the roadstead of Bushire. During my last hours on board, I had an opportunity of witnessing one of those sudden changes in the wind which render the navigation of the Persian Gulf somewhat dangerous for small craft. The prevailing winds are east and northeast. The former is called *Suhaili*, the wind of Canopus; the latter, *Shamâl*, or the north wind simply. Suhaili was blowing mildly while we lay off Bahrein, and during the night it freshened to half a gale. Towards morning it sank a little, but remained in the same quarter till about eight o'clock, when Suhaili all at once gave place to Shamâl, and against a head-wind, with driving rain, the *Rajputana* worked her way up to Bushire. Mr. Paul's steam launch came out to the steamer, and I had the good fortune to be one of the party whom it took ashore. I remember noticing how much greater the cold was than in even high Indian latitudes at this time of year. The strong breeze struck one like a raw April blast bringing showers over the melancholy Irish Sea, while the grey sky and the grey town suggested fleeting thoughts of home.

Bushire is the best-built town on the Persian

coast, and shows some signs of care and improvement. A good sea-wall runs along a great part of its seaward face, and there are small stone quays where a buggalow of sixty or eighty tons can lie and discharge cargo. It is said that an expenditure of 50,000*l.* would enable large ships to approach much nearer to the shore than is possible at present. Long sandy flats and banks extend nearly three miles to sea, but when the tide is out, one can distinguish a channel winding among them, which needs only dredging to make it practicable. A kind of tender, I believe, was made to the Persian Government by an English firm in Bushire some years ago; but the scheme fell through, like most schemes for works of public benefit in Persia. Under proper management, Bushire might be made a place of considerable trade. The customs' duties have been increasing of late years, and are now valued at 60,000 tomans (about 24,000*l.*) a year; but the want of a good road to Shiraz prevents Bushire from assuming the place it is entitled to as a principal feeder of Persia. Had the British Government retained Bushire, after having been at the trouble of capturing it in 1856, the prosperity of the place would no doubt have advanced much more rapidly. Bushire might have been called the eastern Gibraltar; for though there is little outward similarity between the high Spanish rock and the low shores of the Gulf, yet in each case we find a town and harbour at the extremity of a peninsula difficult of access from the mainland, commanding a great highway to India, and of just sufficient extent to be easily defensible. Had we retained Bushire, some arrangement would doubtless have been made with the Persian Government for the improvement of the road to Shiraz. Some embankments remain as memorials of our temporary occupation. A ruined mud fort stands on the edge of the sea. It was defended by a garrison of Arabs in 1856, and its capture by storm cost our troops a loss quite disproportionate to the strength of the position.

Bushire is garrisoned by two companies of infantry and a battery of artillery. The infantry soldiers here, as throughout Persia generally, are slovenly and awkward to the last degree. Their arms are old percussion muskets, all covered with rust. The artillery consists of eight bronze field-guns, in a similar state of uncleanness. Besides these, four carronades or mortars are stowed under cover in the barracks. One

Bushire. 27

of these bears the inscription, "Cast for the Imaum of Muscat by Cyrus Meyer and Co., Boston, 1850." The town has been encompassed by a wall, but the wall has disappeared on the seaward side, and is vanishing on the landward also. The interior of the town presents the customary Eastern labyrinth of narrow and dirty lanes. Viewed, however, from the high ground four miles inland, Bushire is not without its elements of beauty. The city stands clustered together on a low knoll at the point of the peninsula; before it is the sea; behind it extend level sand and swamp; while the remote background is filled with dark and rugged mountains. This is the mountain-chain which was seen behind Bandar Abbas, and again behind Linga; the great barrier which separates the central plateau of Persia from the low strip along the coast.

The Residency buildings are situated at the eastern end of the town, close by the beach. A second or summer Residency stands on the high ground in the inland portion of the peninsula. Hereabouts also are the telegraph buildings, and the house of Mr. Paul, whose generous hospitality afforded me a home during my stay in Bushire. The European society of Bushire is more numerous than that of many an Indian station. The climate is excellent during the winter months, and detestable in summer and autumn. Bushire has an advantage over the ordinary Indian station in enjoying a longer and more bracing period of cold weather. Its great disadvantage is the difficulty of getting away from it,—of going anywhere for change of air and scene. The European residents are glad to welcome a stranger, and treat him magnificently.

CHAPTER II.

BUSHIRE TO SHIRAZ.

FORTY-ONE FARSAKHS: EIGHT DAYS.

I FOUND some difficulty in hiring mules for Shiraz. Bushire had recently been flooded with pilgrims returning from Mecca and Baghdad,— and these worthies had apparently exhausted the resources of the place in the way of transport. The difficulty was increased by the fact that we were a party of four, and all our demands were in the market at the same time, to the no small advantage of the muleteers. My three companions were Messrs. Bruce and Collignon of Ispahan, and a young Scotch lad bent on seeing Persepolis.

18*th February, Shif to Burazjan*, 6 *farsakhs*; 2 *p.m.* to 9.30 *p.m.*—The high road from Bushire to Shiraz has so often been described, that no very minute account of it can be necessary here. It traverses the low coast-region, crosses successive mountain-ranges by successive passes or *kotals*, and finally descends upon the interior plateau of Persia. We left Bushire an hour before noon on the 18th of February. Mr. Paul's steam yacht carried us across the bay to Shif, thus saving two tedious and muddy marches along the coast-line of the peninsula. At Shif, which consists of two huts on a knoll of mud, we found our mules, and after an excellent lunch, provided by my kind host, I began my experience of Persian marching. It was not a happy beginning. Since then I have made a pretty extensive acquaintance with various sorts of Persian roads, in various kinds of weather, but without meeting anything worse than this first march over a clay swamp, on the back of a refractory mule. Burazjun[1] is the first inland station on the Anglo-Persian telegraph, and was destined to be our halting-place for the night. It is about twenty-five miles from Shif; the road draws obliquely away from the coast, leaving the sea on the left hand, and approaching the mountains. In ordinary weather the ground is

[1] Corrupted from Gurazdun, *i.e.*, abode of boars. The place used to be haunted by wild boars before the re-establishment of settled government encouraged the extension of cultivation.

hard clay, mixed with sand; but the rain of the last few days had made the surface slippery and sticky, and had covered it with water. After seven hours of weary plodding, where the only relief to the monotony consisted in watching the varying hues and features of the mountain-wall on the right, we reached Burazjun at half-past nine at night, hungry and tired. Mr. Arshak, who was there in charge of the telegraph station, received us hospitably, and gave us a good dinner.

In the middle of the swamp, we had passed an elegant carriage, which the Prince Governor of Ispahan had ordered out from Europe. It had got so far on its way, by the help of six-and-twenty men, who were painfully bearing it on their shoulders. The wheels and pole had been taken off, and packed in the body of the carriage. How the vehicle has subsequently fared in the kotals, one can only guess. When I left Isfahan nearly four months later, the last news of it was that it was stuck, for the time being, in the neighbourhood of Qazran.

19th February, Kunar-takhta, 8 farsakhs; 8 a.m. to 7 p.m.—Next morning we set out for the telegraph station of Kunar-takhta,[2] nearly

[2] That is, jujube-bed. The Kunar or jujube tree (the common *ber* of Hindustan) is a bush about as large as the

thirty miles north-east of Burazjun. The road wound among the low spurs and knolls in which the first range of mountains sink towards the flat coast-region. Marching in such a country is often tantalizing work; the prospect is bounded by knolls and ridges of which it seems impossible to get clear. But we had a picturesque view of the hills on our right, and the grassy slopes beside the road were bright with celandine, poppy, daisies, and bluebells. At length we rose on the crest of one of these grassy waves, and caught sight of the plain on our left. The broad stony bed of the Dâlaki river, half filled with swift snow-water, wound under miles of date-palm forest, over which again could be seen the bare flats stretching to the sea. On the right hand the hills drew nearer and nearer. Here we began to be conscious of an evil smell, as of sulphuretted hydrogen and coal-tar, proceeding apparently from the plain which had just come in sight. We had heard of the naphtha springs of Dâlaki, and now we were to see them. Sulphur springs are met with first; they well copiously from the base of the hills, and flow across the road.

hawthorn. It flourishes in the neighbourhood of the telegraph station to which it has given its name.

Dalaki. 33

A little further on, the brown naphtha may be seen floating on the white sulphurous waves. Then the village of Dâlaki comes in view. It is only a few mud huts; but the background is formed by hills of various and strange hues. Salt-hills in Persia are always remarkable in shape and colour. They are angular and abrupt, curiously stratified, and coloured red or brown, green, light blue, grey, or white. Behind Dâlaki we could count all these colours, while above all rose the duller brown of the higher ranges in the background. The road enters the salt-hills by a narrow gorge, with fantastic forms of rock on every side. In some places Nature has been playing the architect, and has joined together rocks of different colours, or superimposed slabs of gypsum upon red sandstone, with a neatness which mocks the work of human hands. Winding through defiles and dry watercourses, the road, or rather track, at last comes down upon the Dâlaki river, in the middle of the salt-hills. The river is crossed by a good stone bridge, and the ruins of two older bridges are seen a little way down the stream. Nothing could be wilder than the view from this bridge in the evening sunlight. On either side of the river-bed rise streaked and jagged hills, bright brown, yellow, tawny-red, or grey, while the prospect up-stream is closed by a broken mass of bright red, almost crimson, with the shoulder of a pale green hill just showing itself on the left. Down-stream, the river turns abruptly round the foot of a grey cliff. A solitary square tower at the bridge-head adds to the loneliness of the scene.

The Kotal Malu begins a little beyond this point. It is a rocky staircase a thousand feet high, with its landing in the plain of Khisht, 1800 feet above the sea. It offers some picturesque views of the river, many hundred feet below. Part of the road has been paved with stones, the rest is the work of Nature. The top of the pass is six miles from Kunar Takhta. We reached the telegraph-station at eight in the evening, and were hospitably entertained by Mr. Gifford. The march had been one of about thirty miles, Dâlaki being half-way.

20th February, Kamârij, 3 farsakhs; 9 a.m. to 2 p.m.—Next day we marched only twelve miles to Kamârij. The road traverses a corner of the Khisht plain, leaving rice-fields and date-groves on the left, and enters the low hills which run out from the foot of the Kamârij kotal—a second flight of rocky stairs, 1200 feet high,

Kamárij Kotal.

landing in the quaint little plain of Kamárij, 2950 feet above the sea. There is a slight descent from the summit of the pass into the plain. The kotal itself is remarkable for two things—the singular conformation of the long, flat-topped hills at its base, and the extreme badness of the road. The latter circumstance was partly due to recent floods in the Khisht river, which washes the foot of the kotal. Half-way up, the road becomes so narrow that a laden mule strikes his load against the rocks on either hand. It is literally a staircase, but entirely of Nature's making. It is shut up between overhanging peaks on the left, and a torrent-bed far below on the right. The opposite side of the torrent bed is flanked by a wall of black rock, 300 feet high, furrowed by deep channels worn by the rain of centuries. With one exception, I have seen no mountain pass in Persia so wild and steep as the Kamárij kotal. In the very narrowest part, we met mules descending with bales of cotton. After a wordy war, our servants compelled the muleteers to unload and tumble the bales down the rocks. The unladen mules scrambled out of the way, wherever they could find foothold; and our caravan got past.

Kamârij plain is a level patch, nine miles by four, shut in by hills 600 to 800 feet high. The village has about 500 inhabitants; it lies at the foot of the hills on the left-hand border of the plain, and its grey flat-roofed houses, set in the green of spring, make a pretty picture from a due distance. From the top of the hills, a good view can be had of Kamârij plain and a larger plain to the west, with date-groves and a gleaming river. To the north appear the snowy summits of ranges yet to be crossed.

Our quarters were in the upper room of a small rest-house maintained by the Government for the convenience of European travellers. At this time of the year, when the ground is covered with hoarfrost in the morning, four persons can find accommodation in a small room. In summer it would be a very different matter.

21st *February*, *Qazrân*, 5 *farsakhs*; 7 *a.m.* to 2 *p.m.*—Our next stage was Qazrân. Going down the middle of the Kamârij plain, we made our exit from it over low hills, where the morning air was delightfully fresh and invigorating. Then descending on the upper courses of the Khisht river, whose white bed and blue waters gave colour to the landscape, we left the river on the left, and turned sharp

Qazrân.

to the right (south-eastwards) for the plain of Qazrân. After eight miles of wandering among low ridges, each of which we expected to be the last, we emerged on a view of the level country and the town of Qazrân, lying behind its orange gardens, and at the foot of two green hills. The town is an ancient one, and, like most Persian towns, has seen better days. It may have 8000 inhabitants at present. It suffered severely in the famine of 1879 and 1880. The qanât[3] on which the water supply depends, dried up; many people died, and many more had to leave the place and seek work and food in Bushire or Shiraz. The antiquities of the place are to be found on the green hills behind the town. They consist of some traces of an old fort, and an empty cistern, which supplied the fort with water. The people are proud of their orange gardens, but the oranges are either sour or bitter. Much more noteworthy is the

---

[3] It is hardly necessary to explain that a qanât is an underground conduit formed by excavating a passage which connects the bottoms of a series of wells sunk at intervals of twenty to thirty yards. Water is thus brought from the foot of the mountains, where it may be one hundred feet underground, to plains ten miles distant, where it comes out on the surface.

encouragement recently given to the cultivation of the poppy. The opium trade of Persia will be noticed hereafter; but it may be mentioned here that we were assured that poppy had been introduced into Qazrân within only the last few years, and that the Government, desiring to encourage its cultivation, had exempted poppy fields from the payment of revenue.

22*nd February, Halt at Qazrân.*—In the evening I called on the governor. He received me very courteously in a well-carpeted room, and gave me a chair. His vizier, who was a talkative personage, asked what the English meant to do with Candahar, and evidently thought we were relinquishing it out of pure dread of the Candaharis, of whom he had a high opinion as mighty warriors and "lion-men." He proceeded to express his regrets that Persia was unable to take Herat. "Persia is not a great Power like England," he said. I afterwards found that so judicious an appreciation of Persia's place in the scale of nations is by no means universal throughout the country. After coffee and a qalyan,[4] the

[4] The qalyan is the Persian pipe. It differs from the Indian hookah and the Turkish nargilé in substituting a straight tube, fifteen inches long, for the long flexible tube

governor gave me a guide and lantern to conduct me to the telegraph-office, where we had taken up our quarters.

From Kamârij to Qazrân is about twenty miles. The point where the road turns to the right is about half-way. If, instead of turning to the right, one were to march straight on, the ruins of ancient Shahpur can be reached in less than two hours. Their situation can be descried from the high ground above the Khisht river.

23rd February, Dasht-Arjun, 8 *farsakhs;* 6.30 *a.m. to* 8 *p.m.*—The stage from Qazran to Dasht-Arjun is the best of all in point of scenery, but it is a long day's march—thirty-two miles, with two kotals. The first is called the Kotal Dukhtar, or Maid's Pass; the second, the Pirazan, or Old Woman's. Qazrân plain extends eight miles to the foot of the Kotal Dukhtar. Long grey mountain-walls stretch on either side of the plain. The even line of their summits flushes red in the sunset, and then turns to a dead and ghastly grey. Leaving the plain on the right, the road approaches the

through which the Turk smokes, and the Indian nabob of the past used to smoke. But the lordly Indian hookah has almost disappeared.

left-hand range, enters an amphitheatre of hills, and disappears in a great cleft. There is a path for foot-travellers up the face of the hill. I took this, and was rewarded by a splendid view. The morning air was clear and bracing. At the foot of the hill a caravan was beginning the ascent; I could see the mules picking their way among the rocks, and hear the cries of the muleteers, and the faint jangle of the mulebells. The plain of Qazrân was visible throughout nearly its whole extent. At its lower or eastern end it sinks into a large but shallow lake, which the heavy winter rains had swelled to a length of twelve miles, with a breadth of eight or nine. The hither side of the lake was clothed with brushwood; the farther shores rose in soft green hills. Such a combination of wood, water, and pasture-land is very rare in Persia. In summer, of course, the prospect would lose most of its charms, but as yet the greenness of early spring was fresh and unwithered.

The Kotal Dukhtar is about 1000 feet high. Crossing the mountain-tops, the road descends again into the Dasht-i-Barr, a secluded mountain valley, four miles long by two broad, and full of oak-trees. Though the trees are no great size, and were not yet in leaf, still this

The Kotal Pirazan. 41

part of our march was pretty and pleasant. We rode through a park-like country, with green turf under foot. The valley is closed by the huge mass of the Pirazan. Half-way up is the caravansarai of Mian Kotal. Leaving the mules to follow the windings of the main road, we chose a path which led straight up the rocky mountain-side. It was a hard climb of 2000 feet, and we were all very glad when it was over. The caravansarai is a good one. We easily found a room with a clean stone floor to lunch on. The little level platform on which the caravansarai stands is backed by a magnificent mountain ridge, rising steep and clear into the deep blue of the sky. Dasht-i-Barr lies at one's feet, and snowy peaks fringe the northern horizon. The air is pure, bracing, marvellously clear, and has a remarkable exhilarating and almost intoxicating power.

About two o'clock, we set out again for the second half of the Pirazan. This is longer but less steep than the lower half. Before we reached the top we found ourselves walking in snow. The summit, and the sides of the descent to Dasht-Arjun, are clothed with oak forest. To the right, glimpses are caught of valleys and little plains, sinking by successive steps to the level of Qazrân plain. They are all empty and uninhabited. A little lake, locked in by the untrodden hills, helps to heighten the sense of loneliness. At length Dasht-Arjun comes into view. It is a plain sixteen miles long by ten broad, lying 6600 feet above the sea-level, and shut in by mountains, of which the great ridge of Pirazan (7400 feet) rises the highest, while those at the opposite end are not more than 300 feet above the plain. The centre of the plain is filled by a reedy swamp, which the winter rains had made into a lake of no mean dimensions, and the extreme blueness of its waters called forth admiration from all of us, as we halted for a moment to survey the scene suddenly disclosed at our feet. The plain seemed quite tenantless; but on looking closer we discovered Kala Mushir, a grey mud fort, nearly midway on its level surface, and Dasht-Arjun village was dimly seen at the farther end. Night fell before we reached the telegraph-station. The weariness of the last eight miles was beguiled by watching the light fade behind the snowy mountain-tops, while the stars came out large and full.

We were hospitably welcomed in the telegraph-office, and rejoiced in a warm fire and a good dinner. It froze hard during the night.

Dasht Arjun.   43

As we had only twelve miles to march next day, we had time in the morning to see some of the beauties of Dasht-Arjun.[5] A fine spring breaks out at the foot of a cliff 200 feet high, half a mile from the village. It is associated with the name of a saint, one Shah Mansur, whose shrine stands by the water, under the shade of some tall plane-trees. Some forty feet up the cliff is a small cave, accessible by a ledge. We climbed up, and found it stuck all over with little tin sconces, which had contained votive tapers. I called on the kadkhuda or headman of the village, and was entertained by him with tea and bread and honey, while he answered my questions as to the revenue and agricultural affairs of the village. He told me the well-known story of Colonel St. John's adventure with a lioness on the road down the Pirazan. The beast attacked his horse, and Colonel St. John, after waiting in a tree till the coast was clear, made his way on foot to Kala Mushir. The horse was recovered next morning, with the marks of the brute's claws on his

---

[5] The name means "plain of wild olives." The arjun-tree, or rather shrub, is common in the south of Persia at elevations of 5000 to 6000 feet. It fringes the margin of the lake or swamp in Dasht-Arjun.

hind-quarters. Having told this story, the kadkhuda proceeded to narrate some experiences of his own; among others, of a tussle with a lion, in which he had been bitten in the thigh; and, rolling up his wide Persian trousers, he showed me the scars, which were unmistakable enough. The Persian lion is much smaller than the African lion. It is said to be common enough in the oak forest above Dasht-Arjun. We were told that, two days before, a foot traveller had been turned back by the sight of two of these animals.

24th February, Khan-i-Zanyan, 3 farsakhs; 9 a.m. to 1 p.m.—We started for Khan-i-Zanyan in a snowstorm. The road ascends into the mountain-tops, and winds among them. Under the grey sky, the rounded slopes and summits reminded me of Irish hill-tops of bog and heather. Five miles from Khan-i-Zanyan the road comes down on the Qara-Agâch[6] river,

[6] The name is Turkish, and signifies "black tree." Possibly it may have been suggested by the dark branches of the willows which fill the stony bed of the stream. It is one of the largest rivers of Southern Persia. I crossed it twice again on my way to Lar, the last time almost at the end of its explored course, before it enters the unknown country through which it finds its way to the Persian Gulf.

and crosses it by a stone bridge. The blue and green shades in the water of this swift mountain stream were most vivid and beautiful. Khan-i-Zanyan caravansarai is large and in good repair. We found an excellent room upstairs, with a courtyard. The situation is bleak and exposed, at a height of 6100 feet above the sea-level.

25th February, Shiraz, 8 farsakhs; 5.30 a.m. to 4 p.m.—Next morning early, we saddled our horses for Shiraz. We had thirty-two miles to march, and the road, winding among bare mountain-tops, proved less interesting than any stage since Burazjan. The morning air, however, was very pleasant, keen, and frosty; and the snowy mountains behind us remained in view for the first ten miles, girdling the horizon with a magnificent ring of white peaks. The first view of Shiraz is not striking. The broad, green plain, covered with cultivation, is a welcome sight after the comparatively desolate scenery of the last few days; but the city itself presents nothing to catch the eye. Its three blue domes are not large enough for this purpose. Later in the year the gardens and vineyards which surround the city must help to mark it out from the plain on which it stands;

but when we looked down on Shiraz none of the trees were in leaf. Beyond the plain rise the dark bare mountains, snow-crowned. The knowledge that we beheld an ancient and famous city, that we were approaching a great mart, where all things needful could be bought, and that in a couple of hours we should be welcomed by English people, made up for any want of picturesqueness in the view. We breakfasted in the caravansarai of Chinarâda, and rode rapidly over the last eight miles to Shiraz. Outside the wall we were met by Mr. Fahie of the Telegraph, and by Dr. Odling. Mr. Bruce and I were to be Dr. Odling's guests.

The road from Bushire to Shiraz may be roughly described as running northward as far as Kamarij, and thence eastward to Shiraz. We made seven marches of it, besides one day's enforced halt in Qazrân. It has been travelled in three days, but five days are little enough, with stages as follows:—Burazjan 25 miles, Kunar Takhta 30 miles, Qazrân 32 miles, Dasht-Arjun 32 miles, Shiraz 42 miles.

26th February to 3rd March, Shiraz.—At the time of our visit, Shiraz was governed by one of the Shah's uncles, Prince Firuz Mirza, with the title of Mutamid-ul-Mulk, or Supporter of the Kingdom. By the intervention of Nawab Haidar Ali Khan, who is acting as British Agent and interpreter to the telegraph department, a day and hour were fixed for an interview with the prince. We were ushered into an upper room of the citadel, where the prince was accustomed to transact business. It was almost bare of furniture; chairs, however, were provided for us, and the prince himself took his seat upon a cane-bottomed chair of the humblest description. He was an old man, enveloped in a fur cloak; his manners were extremely courteous, and calculated to set visitors at their ease. The interview lasted about half an hour. The prince questioned us about the state of Europe, the Turkish and Greek questions, and the armaments of the different Powers, in a way which showed considerable acquaintance with these topics on his part. The future of Candahar, the Irish question, Indian superstitions, the Roman Catholic and Protestant religions—were all touched upon. The prince was even familiar with the name of Martin Luther. As to Candahar, he evidently thought that it was relinquished on account of the military difficulty of retaining it. The conversation was entirely in Persian. After the usual tea, qalyan, and coffee, we took our leave.

Prince Firuz Mirza has the reputation of being a severe governor. The old man's face had lines in it which seemed to express energy and resolution. It is perhaps hardly fair to draw his character from such imperfect information as I obtained, chiefly from his subjects and his enemies. Still, a brief sketch of a Persian Governor may possess some interest, though it ought to be taken with charitable qualifications. The province of Fars was in a disturbed state when Firuz Mirza assumed the government of Shiraz. He reduced it to order by measures of great but perhaps wholesome severity. After many real or reputed robbers had been crucified or buried in mortar-pits, the roads became safe, and have remained safe during his administration. But in revenue matters, perhaps the prince has been less successful. The peasantry, at least, wherever I spoke to them on the subject, were loud in their complaints. Since Firuz Mirza's accession, they said, *Fars tamám shud*, the province had been done for. The revenues, exacted with rigour in years of famine, have been spent on the shrines of Karbala and Qazimain near Baghdad. Besides, the prince is said to have vastly increased his private fortune during his term of government. Since his recall he has been detained in Teheran on a charge of arrears in the provincial revenues.

The story of Shaikh Mazkur, of Kangun, illustrates the alleged severity and greed of the prince. Kangun is a small maritime settlement on the coast of Persian Biluchistan. A friend of the Shaikh got into trouble, and the Shaikh was invited to ransom him. He did so, but the man was nevertheless put to death. Next year, the Shaikh deducted the amount of the ransom from the revenue paid by him to Shiraz. The prince sent his servants to collect the revenue in full. They seized and carried away a boy of the tribe, for purposes familiar to Persians. The Shaikh recovered the lad by force. He was now declared a rebel, and after sustaining a long siege in his hill-fort, he surrendered himself on a promise of personal safety, confirmed by an oath on the Koran. The oath, of course, was violated; the Shaikh was carried to Shiraz, and brought into the city on an ass, with every circumstance of ignominy and insult, in the presence of the whole of the garrison, and of the populace. A few days later he was strangled in the parade-ground of the citadel, and the body was suspended by hooks under the chin to a gallows erected in the square, and derisively inscribed with the name of the Shaikh's fort. The gallows was standing while I was in Shiraz. The prince advised me to travel to Kangun, to "the fort he had conquered," if I wanted to see an interesting part of the country.

Two days suffice to exhaust the sights of Shiraz. The bazaar built by Karim Khan, about a hundred and fifty years ago, is in the form of a cross, with a dome at the intersection of the arms. The length of the main branch is 500 yards; that of the cross-branch 120. The roof is vaulted, and 22 feet high; the roadway 12 feet broad; and the shops which open back from the masonry platforms on either side are neat and well stocked. It is a better bazaar than can be found in many Indian towns of much greater size. The Masjid-i-Nau, though called the new mosque, is the oldest mosque in Shiraz. It consists of flat-roofed cloisters built round a fine courtyard paved with stone; the lower course of the cloisters are also of stones. The mosque of Shah Chiragh is conspicuous by its blue dome, the lower portion of which is adorned with conventional patterns in black, white, blue, and yellow. The height of the building, from base to finial, is about 110 feet. Sayyid Husain's mosque, in the western quarter of the city, is of about the same size, but in worse repair. Shah Chiragh has rich endowments. An English lady recently had the courage to enter this mosque, disguised like the Persian woman who accompanied her. The interior is rich with lamps of gold and silver, doors plated with those metals, &c. On the gateway of the Vakil's mosque, and of an old college, there still remain beautiful specimens of flowering designs in enamelled tiles of the old style. The art has partly been lost. Nothing could exceed the grace and beauty of form and colour shown in this workmanship of a century ago.

Outside the city are various gardens, which we visited, though all the trees, except the cypress, were bare. The best is the Bagh-i-Takht, or terrace-garden. It is built in terraces against the slope of a hill. Its upper end is crowned by a two-storied building, fantastic and not ungraceful. The grounds fall away from the portal in a succession of broad terraces, down which a stream with waterfalls used to flow in a stone-paved channel, filling a large stone basin or tank on one of the terrace levels. But the property—it belongs to the Shah—has been much neglected; the house is falling to ruin, and the stream and tank are dry. Neglect and decay are indeed the common features of crown property all over Persia.

The most remarkable relics of antiquity near Shiraz are three wells on a rocky hill, two miles north-east of the city. Nobody knows who made them. Probably they are older than the Mohammedan conquest. The hill is about 500 feet high, and very steep. It seems to be composed of sandstone and limestone. Two of the wells are on the side facing the city. These are the deepest. The mouth of the larger of the two is about seven feet by five, and its depth is nearly 500 feet.[7] The shaft evidently sinks through the whole depth of the hill. It is hewn in the solid limestone, and very smoothly cut; the sides are perfectly plumb, and a stone dropped from the centre of the mouth will reach the bottom without

---

[7] Repeated experiments showed that a stone took just six seconds to reach the bottom. Allowing half a second for the sound to come up, the depth would be 484 feet.

Shiraz. 53

striking anywhere on its way. Far down, one hears the cooing of invisible pigeons, and a shower of stones makes them flap about with a noise like distant thunder. The third well, at the back of the hill, has seats or ledges cut in the rock above it. Remains of old fortifications encompass the summit of the hill. From the topmost peak the whole plain of Shiraz can be seen, and the salt lake of Mahalu, twenty miles to the east. The plain is well watered, fertile, and green, and miles of orchards cover its western end. Shiraz city is a compact brown area in the green landscape, overhung with smoke, and adorned by three blue domes.

While in Shiraz, I had the good fortune to be invited to an Armenian banquet. It was a magnificent entertainment. We sat down, thirty in number, on either side of a long table-cloth, spread on the floor, and covered with various kinds of *pilau* and other dishes, including a lamb roasted whole. Beer and Shiraz wine flowed freely. The dinner was followed by drinking of healths. A dignitary of the Armenian church, second in rank (I believe) to the bishop, who had come from Isfahan to grace the occasion, was the principal speech-maker. He preferred cherry brandy of terrific strength, and with the decanter affectionately grasped and held in his ample lap, among the folds of his black cassock, while the other hand held the glass ready for the generous liquor, he delivered several speeches in Armenian, with evident eloquence, and not without dignity and grace. The custom is that the person whose health is proposed should acknowledge the honour in a song while the company are drinking, and afterwards return thanks in prose. Armenian songs are not unlike Gregorian chants. Our ecclesiastical dignitary kept up a deep running bass that would have done credit to the drones of a couple of bagpipes. The whole thing was excellent fun, and had that heartiness and kindliness about it which mixed Indian entertainments so woefully want.

CHAPTER III.

PERSEPOLIS.

3rd March, Zarghun.—As my route from Shiraz would not lead in the direction of Persepolis, and as it seemed a pity to let slip an opportunity of seeing such a famous place, I determined to spend four days in an excursion thither, the more so as I should fortunately have a companion in young Mr. Gray. We left Shiraz on the 3rd of March, and halted at Zarghun, which is twenty miles from Shiraz, and half-way to Persepolis. The road winds among the mountains which form the northern wall of the Shiraz plain. They are stony, and the road is stony; there is no view, and we were glad to come at last upon the descent to the plain of Bâjgah.[1] This is only a mile in

---

[1] Videlicet, "taxing-place." There is a caravansarai here, but I am not sure whether the toll-house which gave the place its name exists still, or whether the tolls are taken at Shiraz gate.

breadth, and the ascent on its farther side leads to the lower slopes of the hills which border the plain of Zarghun. After some six miles among these stony undulations, the whole plain discloses itself, with Zarghun town most quaintly situated at the foot of a great ridge of rock, a thousand feet high, brown and bare, and seemingly inaccessible. In fact, however, it can be ascended anywhere with but little difficulty, and the view repays the labour of the climb. The plain immediately below, occupied by the well-watered fields of Zarghun and its villages, is good cultivated country, and the slopes of the lower hills are dotted with vineyards. To the left the plain runs up into a bay between narrowing mountain-ranges; to the right it stretches away in a broad expanse, which, when we looked upon it, was a great sheet of water, made by the winter rains. A ring of snowy ridges hemmed in the prospect all round; their sides and summits flushed red in the sunset, and then turned white, while the water showed a cold steely blue. The few villages, in their mud-built brownness, were lost in the widespread bareness of the plain; and if the eye turned from these vast empty spaces, it rested on the rocky ledges of the broad hill-side.

4th March, Puza.—Next day we marched to Puza chaparkhana or post-house. The first three miles are traversed by the aid of a stone causeway and bridges, carrying the road over the flooded plain. All the rest is level dry clay, with but one incident to interrupt its monotony, a poetical sort of incident, namely, the calm Bendemeer, with its roses and nightingales. This delightful river is nowadays indistinguishable from the ordinary Indian *nullah* in the rains. The water is muddy, and flows with tortuous course between muddy banks. As for the rose and the bulbul, "one might as well hunt half a day for a forgotten dream." Crossing the river by a stone bridge, and marching ten miles across the plain of Marvdasht, we came in sight of Persepolis two miles on our right, while the tombs could be seen in the face of the rocks four miles to our left front. From the Bendemeer, Puza chaparkhana seems to be five miles distant. It is really twelve. The clear, dry air of Persia has a marvellous effect in shortening distances to the eye.

The tombs and Persepolis are on opposite sides of the plain, which here begins to narrow between spurs of the mountains which bound it on the north. Persepolis stands at the foot of the eastern spur. The tombs are carved in the face of the cliffs of the western spur. In the upper part of the spur these cliffs are 500 feet high; but the lower portion, in which the tombs have been excavated, sinks from 200 feet to 90. The tombs are five in number. The door of each is forty feet from the ground, but the cutting into the rock extends twenty feet below the door, and twenty feet above. In preparing their sepulchres the first thing the old Persian monarchs did was to carve a huge cross on the face of the cliff, with its lateral arm rather longer and broader than the upright one. The cutting, at the base of the cross, is six feet deep; where the lateral arm crosses the upright it is three feet deeper; and the rock overhangs the head of the cross in heavy masses, and juts out along the sides. The foot of the cross is twenty feet from the ground. One can scramble up to this point, where the six-foot ledge affords ample resting-place; but to climb twenty feet more to the three-foot ledge before the door of the tomb is not such an easy matter. Only one of the five tombs is accessible, and that by the help of a rope. As we were looking up in perplexity, a villager came and offered to pull us up for a consideration. He himself climbed the face of the rock, and, letting down his black rope of camel's hair, hauled up Gray first, as being the lighter, and then Gray and he landed me also on the ledge, and we were free to enter the tomb. The doorway is six feet by three. Inside, a transverse gallery extends five yards to the right and fifteen to the left, and opening back from it are three recesses, each of which was the resting-place of three kings. The bodies of the kings have long been taken away, and the broken slabs that covered them lie on or in each empty sarcophagus. The gallery is dark and full of bats. From the ledge outside one looks over the wide plain, stretching beyond the mountain-spurs as far as eye can see. Behind, to the right hand and the left, extends the smooth wall of rock; and above, near the top of the cross, stands the graven effigy of a king, bow in hand, worshipping fire burning on an altar. The sun hangs over the altar, and midway between the king and the fire a winged figure hovers in the air. Over all broods the spirit of silence and immemorial desolation. No sign of life or movement can be discerned on the plain below, any more than in the rock-hewn and tenantless chambers of the dead.

It was a relief to stand on the ground again, and turn to the tablets sculptured along the foot of the rocks. These represent equestrian combats, on a gigantic scale, most spiritedly executed; and one huge carving portrays the submission of Valerian to Shapur. The Persian King is mounted, while the humbled Roman kneels before him, arrayed in true Roman garb, the tunic with cloak fastened by the fibula over the shoulder. A long inscription in Pahlavi seeks to perpetuate the victor's triumph; but it has never, I believe, been deciphered, and is partly illegible now. A still less legible legend in Greek is inscribed below the charger; one can spell out *ABPA*, and two *Θ*; the rest is blurred and lost.

A few yards from the foot of the cliff stands a square building of white marble, thirty-five feet high, containing a single square chamber, entered by a door eight feet above the ground. It is marked on the exterior by oblong indentations, carved apparently for ornament. They are a foot in vertical length, and about three inches broad, and cover the walls, giving the building a strange appearance from a distance. The large marble blocks of which this ancient fire-temple is composed are admirably hewn, and most neatly compacted together. Two huge slabs, twenty-one feet long by seven broad, form the ceiling of the room; but the upper surface of the roof is composed of four such slabs, each five feet broad and a foot thick. One of these was partly displaced by an earthquake ten years ago. Its edge now overhangs the roof to the breadth of eighteen inches. In no other respect does the building show any damage save below the door, where the destroying hand of man has dug out some of the marble blocks. So new and fresh does this strange temple look, that on first approaching it, before its antique massiveness has been perceived, one thinks it a watch-tower or guardhouse, built recently for some custodian of the tombs. As evening fell we turned away from these monuments of forgotten priests and kings, and walked back to the chaparkhana, passing on our way a marble platform on the plain—a halting-place, perhaps, in funeral processions of royalty two thousand years ago.

Next morning we rode to Persepolis. The ruins of Persepolis have been described by skilled antiquarians, so that any attempt of mine to give a scientific account of them would be at once unnecessary and presumptuous. Still, I may perhaps try to explain what the casual visitor may expect to see in this famous place. It has already been said that Persepolis stands at the foot of the rocky spur which confines the northern end of Marvdasht plain on its eastern side. This spur sinks into the plain, a shelving slope of brown rock. From the foot of the slope a huge stone platform has been built out into the plain. It is 312 yards broad, and extends 500 yards along the foot of the hill. The surface of the platform being level, its height above the ground varies according to the configuration of the broken country on which it stands. On the north side the ground rises so nearly to the level of the platform, that by the help of ruins and *débris* which have filled up the interval, a horse is able to scramble up. But on the western side, one looks down forty feet of sheer wall, and the height is even greater on the south. The western face is rendered accessible at its highest point by a magnificent double staircase. Each step is seven yards broad, and so gentle is the ascent, that a horse can be ridden up or down. It is these royal stairs which have won the largest tribute of admiration from writers on Persepolis; but

Persepolis. 63

they seemed to us less remarkable than the remains of ancient grandeur to be seen on the platform itself. The stairs lead up to the grand portal, between two gigantic marble bulls, whose pedestals bear names without number, some of note, as Malcolm, Pottinger, Ferrier, or even Stanley, *New York Herald*, 1870. It would be well if these were the only defacements and indignities which the ruins of Persepolis have had to suffer. Passing between the bulls, one comes to a space which had four marble columns. Two only are standing. Beyond them is another pair of bulls, facing the opposite way, that is, towards the hill-side. This is all that remains of the grand portal. It gave access to a double flight of steps, leading up a second platform, which rises nine feet above the main platform, and presents a face richly adorned with triumphal and sacrificial processions, sculptured in the smooth black syenite. At the top of the steps stood a transverse colonnade of twelve marble pillars, in two rows of six each; behind that a wall with gates; and then a hall fifty yards square, its roof supported by thirty-six pillars in six rows of six. On the right hand and the left were colonnades of twelve pillars. Of these seventy-two pillars twelve[2] only are standing, and not one of the twelve is perfect, yet they stand sixty feet high, and though their symmetry is sometimes severely tried by capitals of undue depth and heaviness, still the stateliness and beauty of the fluted shafts of white marble rise victorious over defects of conception and ravages of time. This was the great hall, the chief glory of the Persian kings. Moving from the grand portal the traveller crosses the great hall in a direction parallel to the hill-side, and finds himself before a third step in the platform, which being ascended, he enters the ruins of the hall known as that of Darius.[3] Here there are no traces of

[2] Mr. Binning, of the Madras Civil Service, who visited Persepolis in 1852, found thirteen pillars standing. The capital of one so far overhung the shaft that Mr. Binning was half afraid it would topple over on him while he was taking his measurements. Since then the earthquake shock which displaced part of the roof of the fire-temple at the tombs has thrown down the thirteenth pillar, but the overhanging capital still remains—"wonder to all who do the same espy."

[3] Mr. Binning gives the dimensions of the various halls. The breadth of the great hall, taken at right angles to the hill-side, is stated as 127 yards. I could reckon only 98 yards from edge to edge of the outer colonnades, but Mr. Binning probably measured to the edge of the platform. The central group of 36 pillars, which seems to have had a

columns, but the walls which surrounded the hall are still standing. They are of massive black syenite. The stone bears a high polish. One of the many blank windows of this hall has been polished till it reflects images like a mirror. Going on in the same direction, and surmounting another step or grade in the platform, the traveller reaches the hall of Xerxes. The walls are partly standing, and the bases and foundations of columns can be traced on the floor; they were thirty-six pillars, in six rows of six. But these were much smaller than the lofty columns of the great hall. Judging by the walls, the roof could not have been much more than twenty-five feet high. They were of black syenite. From the edge of the platform on which this palace stands, one looks down on the floor of the main platform, twenty-five feet below, and wonders at the height to which one has insensibly mounted, and at the marvellous masonry which looks almost as fresh and sound as if the giant stones had been laid yesterday.

Hitherto we have supposed the traveller to be moving *parallel* to the hill-side. If he turns

---

roof of its own, measures 50 yards square. The hall of Darius is shown by Mr. Binning as 60 yards long and 32 broad; the hall of Xerxes as 33 yards square.

now, and moves *towards* the hill-side, that is, towards the back of the main platform, he will enter the hall called that of the hundred columns. This was a square of ten columns by ten. Each side of the square measures about eighty yards, and the remains of the walls which enclosed it suggest a height of about forty feet for the roof. Last year the Ihtisham ud Daulat,[4] urged by the well-known Persian scholar and antiquarian, Dr. Andreas, made extensive excavations in this part of Persepolis, laying bare the bases of all the hundred columns, and revealing the remains of their shafts and capitals, broken and buried in earth. The columns stood on inverted lotus-flowers, beautifully carved. They have preserved all their smoothness and freshness under the ruins of a thousand years. The hard black stone renders faithfully every graceful curve and clear-cut line entrusted to it by the chisel of the fire-worshipping stonecutter. Nay more, behind this hall, up the hill-side, one finds the stonecutting yard itself, with the quarry above. The slope is covered with chipped fragments. Above this again is the reputed tomb of Darius.

[4] Or "Majesty of the State." He is the son of Prince Firuz Mirza, late Governor of Shiraz, and was Governor of Bihbahan during his father's administration.

It is like those on the opposite side of the plain, but easily accessible. An admirable view of Persepolis can be had from its gloomy portal. The lines of the ruined halls can be traced, the very pillars counted, and the whole plan of the place lies open to the eye.

The face of the minor platform which supports the hall of Darius is profusely adorned with figures, executed with no mean degree of art. Where protected from the barbarity of Mussulman zeal, they are as bold and distinct as if they were the work of to-day. Especially noticeable are a horse and chariot, a two-humped Bactrian camel, and a sacrificial procession of bulls and rams, with a led horse bringing up the rear. The chief priest mounts the steps of the shrine with a kid in his arms; his attendants follow, bearing baskets. In the doors and on the walls are figures of kings and warriors—larger than life—of priests in ceremonial robes, or of winged spirits. Everywhere the stonework is of the most massive and perfect description. A polished corner-stone of the hall of Darius is eight feet by four feet by five, and it is joined to its fellow with a neatness of which modern architects might be proud. Conscientiousness and solidity of work characterized the builders of Persepolis. Mr. Arthur Arnold in his work "Through Persia by Caravan," expresses a doubt whether the columns of Persepolis were not hollow, or filled with wood. Mr. Arnold had not the advantage of seeing the recent excavations, which, by unearthing countless fragments of columns, have proved conclusively that there was no hollowness of the kind. The thorough goodness of the work is testified by the clearness of the arrow-headed inscriptions on a fallen block from the hall of Darius. They seem to be fresh from the chisel. On one of the panels of the hall are two long inscriptions in praise of Nasir ud Din Shah, cut three years ago by order of a loyal money-changer of Shiraz. They are less clear and bold than the record carved in praise of King Darius.

In situation, Persepolis is most forlorn. Before it is the wide emptiness of Marvdasht; behind it, the desolation of the bare hill-side. Though designed on so huge a scale, it has to be searched for in the vast landscape of which it is the smallest feature. As if by the irony of Nature, the work of monarchs is dwarfed and outbraved by three castles of Nature's building, planted on the distant plain. They are three hills,[5] rising 700 feet with steep smooth slope, and then crowned with a wall of crags 300 feet high. It is these gigantic objects which seem the proper guardians of Marvdasht; and to look towards them from Persepolis awakens thoughts of the vanity of human greatness. Commonplace moralizing is distasteful enough; but even the most commonplace person could hardly visit Persepolis without feeling some touch of genuine pity and reverence. The immense solidity of the ruins, and yet their fragility; the clear-cut and beautiful inscriptions, vainly trying to tell their tale in a language once used by the rulers of half Asia, but long since silent and forgotten; the stately effigies of kings sunk ages ago in "death's dateless night;" and around all the vast silence of the plain, and the snowy mountain-tops, unchanged themselves, the secular watchers over so many changes—all these send their influence forth, and unconsciously subdue the soul. Keats sought to express the sensations stirred in him by the sight of the Elgin marbles in the sonnet beginning,—

[5] Binning gives their names as Istakha, Shahrak, Kum-Firuz. The only names I could ascertain for two of them were Ghila and Ghilau.

"My spirit is too weak ; mortality
Weighs heavily on me, like unwilling sleep—"

and it is some such feeling as this which steals over the mind of the wanderer among the fallen columns and broken walls which cover the noble platform of Persepolis.

CHAPTER IV.

SHIRAZ TO FIRUZABAD.

TWENTY FARSAKHS; FOUR DAYS.

6th to 9th March, Shiraz—By this time I had settled upon a route for my future travels. I would march from Shiraz to Lar, by way of Firuzabad, and from Lar directly to Karman. This promised to include some country imperfectly laid down in my maps.[1]

Mules were not easily found. The Indian Government had been buying up mules for transport service; and the season of the year was one when muleteers prefer to loiter along the road to Bushire, letting their cattle graze on the rich grass of the roadside. At last I got five mules for 15 francs (*qirans*) a day.

[1] My maps were that of the Surveyor-General of India, showing the countries between India and Asiatic Russia, corrected up to 1878, and Colonel St. John's large map of Persia, published by the Surveyor-General in 1876. The former is on a scale of thirty-two miles, the latter on one of sixteen miles to the inch.

9th March, Deh-i-Nau, 4 farsakhs; 1.20 p.m. to 5.20 p.m.—On the 9th of March I bade farewell to Dr. Odling's hospitable house, and started with five mules for Deh-i-Nau. The prince had provided me with a *ghulam* or mounted and armed attendant—an old man whose life had been passed in such service, and whose horse and arms were apparently coeval with himself. His steed was white and devoid of spirit; by great exertions, however, it could be shaken into a kind of shuffling trot. His arms were a brace of pistols, and a single-barrelled gun with a round Persian stock. Besides this worthy, whose name was Zaki Beg, I had two Persian lads as cook and groom. The two muleteers raised the number of my train to five; and last, but greatest, came the portly Sayyid Ali, now my only travelling-companion. He had already begun to exercise his wit by giving the name of *the modern Joseph* to the younger muleteer, a singularly ill-favoured youth; Joseph being proverbial among Musalmans for his miraculous beauty.

Having only four farsakhs[2] to march, we did not set out till the afternoon. The road runs

[2] A farsakh is about four miles. About Bushire, and in other parts of the south, it is three miles only; but, as a rule, it may be reckoned at four miles, and sometimes is more nearly five. From Isfahan to Teheran is a distance

The Shiraz Plain. 73

very nearly south, across the plain of Shiraz. Villages and gardens enclosed by high mud walls are seen at various distances. After eight miles the plain began to grow swampy. Its drainage is towards the salt lake (Darya-i-Mahalu) which forms its eastern border; but the water collects also in a hollow under the hills which limit the plain on its western side, and the heavy winter rains had left more water here than usual. The edges of this swamp abound with snipe. Dr. Odling told me he has shot as many as twenty couple in an afternoon. Ducks are plentiful in the interior, but the reeds and underwood render shooting difficult. Leaving the swamp on the right hand, the road crosses the stream by which its overflow reaches the lake. Beyond the bridge the road divides. One branch goes westwards to the margin of the lake, here some six miles distant, and thence south-westwards, between the lake and the Mahalu mountains, to a place called Fasa, which, though seventy miles distant, has given its name to the bridge. The other, which was our route, holds on in a direction nearly south, keeping the Mahalu range on the east, that is, on

of 268 miles by the telegraph line. The road, which is not so straight, is reckoned at seventy farsakhs, i.e., almost exactly four miles to the farsakh.

the left hand. The point of divergence of the Fasa and Firuzabad roads, in fact, is at the head of the Mahalu range, where the mountains sink into the plain in the shape of stony hills capped by solitary rocks, which some process of weathering has worn into the shape of an inverted egg-cup.

We reached Deh-i-Nau an hour before sunset. It is a walled village of the type common in Persia—four mud walls and four mud towers, one at each angle. The length of a side is about 100 yards. Entering by the eastern gate, through a long passage built over by upper rooms, the only thing I could see at first was the splendour of the purple evening sunlight on the lofty and rugged sides of the Sabz-Poshan mountain, directly west. The effect was enchanting for a moment; one seemed to be riding into a vast shadowy vault. But these sky-born glories soon gave place to the mud-built squalor of the village, and as we emerged from the gateway, a chorus of dogs protested against our intrusion. The Persian village dog is not unlike a shaggy and short-nosed Scotch collie. The animals having been quieted, Sayyid Ali called for the headman (Kadkhuda), and producing the letter which had been given

me by the prince, demanded lodgings for the
night. The Kadkhuda looked blank enough,
till it was explained to him that we meant to
pay for everything. He gave me an upper
room, nine feet square by six and a half high,
and found me a couple of chickens for dinner.
I had also the pleasure of a conversation with
him and his satellites—a doleful discourse on
the tyranny of the Governor of Shiraz, and of
the Qavvâm, who owns most of the villages
hereabouts. In most large cities of Persia,
there will be found a titled individual who,
though not in fact an official, combines the
characters of large landowner, farmer of the
public revenues, and man of local influence.
Such men become for a time the virtual
governors of a province or part of a province.
They are then squeezed, or their power passes
away by death; and another arises to follow
their fortune and their fate. Such was the
Mushîr of Shiraz in a bygone generation. He
has left memorials in the bridges and noble
caravansarais on the Bushire and Shiraz road,
and in a fine caravansarai adjoining the main
bazaar of Shiraz city. In his place, at present,
is the Qavvâm.[3] "I paid 500 tomans to the

---

[3] Mushîr means "Counsellor;" Qavvâm, "Upholder."

Qavvâm last year," said the Kadkhuda, "all pure extortion. I have not the value of three tomans in my house. The land is good enough, if it were not for tyranny. Whom have we to appeal to? Fars has been ruined since the Mutamid ud Daulat came to Shiraz." The Kadkhuda proved to be pretty well up in domestic politics, though entirely ignorant of the Afghan war, and, indeed, of the existence of Afghans. He asked me the latest news of the quarrel between Shaikh Obaidullah and the Shah (the Kurdish inroad of 1880-81), and whether it was true that the Zill us Sultan was coming to Shiraz in Prince Firuz Mirza's place. I had heard something of the latter rumour from Dr. Odling; it subsequently proved to be correct.

10*th March, Kavar*, 6 *farsakhs*; 9 *a.m.* to 4 *p.m.*—They unbarred the gates of Deh-i-Nau at six o'clock next morning, and drove their cattle afield—poor black cattle; I have hardly seen poorer in India. The ground was covered with hoarfrost, and the air very cold. Our caravan did not get under way till half-past eight. Our road still pointed southward. We marched seven miles through the southern end of the Shiraz plain. Irrigation here is from wells—a rare thing in Persia — but the accumulated drainage, as the plain sinks lower, brings the water to within a few feet of the surface.

The Mahalu mountains were still on our left. Seven miles from Deh-i-Nau, they throw out a low spur, which divides the plain of Shiraz from that of Kavar. It is crossed by a road called Baba Haji's Pass[1] (*gardana i Baba Haji*), and there is also an easier road which turns the point of the spur, and which is used by the Qavvâm's carriage, when he takes his drives abroad. His son had lately been shooting in Kafr and Jahrum, and the tracks of his carriage wheels were still visible on the road. Following the upper road, we passed a ruined caravansarai with some fine elm-trees, and beheld above us a pillar of lime, the size of a man. Zaki Beg hastened to inform us that the pillar contained the mortal remains of one Ali Dad, a notorious robber, whose career was cut short by his being encased alive in mortar on this spot, by order of the prince, the year before last. He stands

[1] I regret that I failed to discover who this worthy was. The difference between a *gardana* and a *kotal* usually is, that while the kotal goes straight up a mountain, the gardana deals chiefly with low hills, and if it has to cross a mountain, works its way obliquely along the side, and dodges over some convenient saddle-back.

there now like Lot's wife turned into a pillar of salt. While utterly repudiating the theory—sometimes advanced even by European residents in Persia—that the country could not be kept in order without recourse to such inhuman punishments, I am nevertheless bound to admit that it was much pleasanter to meet with Ali Dad in that harmless and picturesque position than if he had stopped the road of my caravan with his ragged rascals. Let me also say, however, that for the European traveller in Persia the roads are almost invariably safe, and that brigandage generally is much exaggerated by rumour. It will be seen hereafter how groundless were the rumours of robbers which were heard at a few points in my travels.

Crossing the gardana, which may be 150 feet high, we descended into the plain of Kavar. This is watered by the Qara-Agach river, the same as we had crossed near Khan-i-Zanyan, on our way to Shiraz. But the river is barred from Shiraz by the mountains which guard the Shiraz plain on the west; so it turns south-eastward, and, flowing under these mountains, at last reaches the end of the range, bends eastward, and enters the Kavar plain through a defile between the end of this range and the beginning of another. Here, from time immemorial, a stone dam has supplied water to the the canal which irrigates the Kavar plain. The legendary and heroic monarch Bahman is said to have been the original maker. In Fath Ali Shah's time (early in the present century) the dam was carried away, and was rebuilt for 4000 tomans. This, of course, represents principally the price of materials, most of the labour being obtained free from the villages that live by the water. This winter the dam had broken again, and all the water-channels were dry. The Qavvâm had already begun to repair the damage. Neither dam nor river can be seen from the road; the mouth of the defile is six miles distant on the right, and the river is so deep sunk as to be invisible till its banks are reached. The plain is level, and studded with camel-thorn, and has villages at long intervals. The southern part collects the drainage and produces rice. We turned aside to a village fort to eat our mid-day meal, sending on Zaki Beg to provide a place swept and garnished, and some drinking-water. At the gate we were met by Zaki Beg, in perplexity. "The sons of burnt fathers," he said, "have all run away; I can find only an old woman." 1

found my way into a stable, and while I was eating my lunch there, some of the inhabitants took heart and returned, and brought me water. They complained bitterly of oppression, and foretold ruin to the crops from the breaking of the dam.

Kavar itself was eight miles farther, a large village surrounded by orchards. I went to the caravansarai, but was immediately invited by a landlord of part of the village to put up in a house which he was building. I found my new quarters exceedingly comfortable, and my host talkative and friendly. He gave me an excellent dinner. He lamented the state of Persia, the absence of public works, the corruption of the officials, the neglect of education, and the condition of the army. England and Russia, he said, might divide Persia between them whenever they pleased.

There is a small cluster of villages in the neighbourhood of Kavar, but by far the greater part of the plain—it is twenty miles long by twelve broad—is uncultivated and desolate. A river in Persia by no means implies irrigation. Most Persian rivers, like the Qara-Agach here, are so deep sunk that the water cannot be brought to the level of the fields.

A Persian Police-inspector. 81

11*th March, Jawakan,* 5 *farsakhs;* 8.30 *a.m.* to 3.30 *p.m.*—Next morning we turned directly south, and crossed the river, here running south-east, by a stone bridge thirty feet above the water. The Qara-Agach here is a mountain stream, barely fordable; but it has less water in ordinary seasons. On the farther side rises the Safidâr range, 2000 feet high, still capped with snow. This we crossed by a defile opening unexpectedly between cliffs 150 feet high. It is called the pass of Gur Bahman, or Bahman's tomb. The tomb is a barrow of stones in the mouth of the defile. Our party to-day had been augmented by a *Zabit* of *tufangchis,* a kind of uncivilized police officer, who was journeying to our next stage, Khwaji. He was a smart and rather handsome youth, well armed and accoutred, mounted on a half-Arab pony, and, as Sayyid Ali remarked, considered himself a second Rustam. He entertained us with stories of blood-feuds, illustrating the desperate and implacable character of the tribes he had to keep in order; with panegyrics of the valour and enterprise of various robbers, including the *mortared* Ali Dad; and with the praises of his own thirty tufangchis, each of whom was equal to ten ordinary men, and also possessed the valuable faculty of walking up perpendicular rocks. Two of these ragged fellows we saw as we entered the pass. They stood 200 feet above us, on the rugged slope of the hill, and discharged their rusty guns, to which the Zabit replied by letting off his. The pass gradually widened as we ascended, and finally opened out on the mountain ridge, and disclosed a tiny valley on the farther side, two miles long by three quarters of a mile broad. Like the mountain-side sloping down to it, this dell was covered with almond, wild olive, and mastich-trees (*bana*). A solitary fort stood in the middle, recently built for a garrison of ten tufangchis, who cultivate a little wheat, and receive precarious pay. The Dasht-i-Muak (so this dell is called) is watered by a spring which breaks out of a cleft in the rocks a little to the left of the road by which we descended. The brook makes its escape at the farther end of the dell. Above the dell, embosomed in mountain-tops, wide green valleys stretch aloft in untrodden loneliness. Beyond the Dasht-i-Muak the stream falls into a ravine, under a huge precipitous hill. The road follows the water. We lunched at the mouth of the ravine, near a tower held by a few tufangchis, and then entered the ravine. The road soon disappeared, and we had to make our way down the channel of the stream, among pools, waterfalls, and blackberry bushes, and between overhanging cliffs 200 feet high. It was pleasant and cheerful work, though I was not without anxiety for the mules. We came out above the Khwaji plain, passed Zanjiran on our right—a well-built mud fort on a stony mound—and sought quarters in Jawâkân, the nearest village on the plain. The Kadkhuda lodged us in a suite of empty rooms, well plastered, and furnished with doors; I believe they were used for religious services during the Muharram and on holidays. I was very glad of a fire. After dinner the Kadkhuda came in and smoked a pipe, and talked about revenue matters.

12th March, Firuzabad, 6 farsakhs; 8.30 a.m. to 5 p.m.—The next day's march was to take us to Firuzabad. The road passes through two defiles, cloven by the river in a rocky ridge 500 feet high, called the Knife-edge *(par-i-Kârd)*, and in a mountain-range beyond. The intermediate valley sends two affluents to swell the stream, which has already been augmented by two more in the Khwaji plain, and the result for us was that the second defile was full of water and impracticable, and we were obliged to climb over the mountains, instead of going through them with the river. I was sorry, for the defile has some fine scenery, besides many specimens of ancient rock-sculptures. But the disappointment was partly compensated by a fine view from the top of the mountain. Behind us were snowy summits and unpeopled valleys, a broad domain of grass and rock, swept by mountain-winds; but before us and far below us spread the spacious plain of Firuzabad, a summer scene of gardens and villages, and fair green fields. We descended thitherward over rocky slopes paved with great flat slabs, often strangely resembling the work of human hands, and forming natural roads eight or ten feet broad, with the shelving hill-side above, and a small precipice below. All that had been done by man was to clear away the loose stones. At length we came on the green levels of the plain, and rode four miles past broad fields of wheat, and by the side of watercourses. In the genial afternoon sunlight the well-cultivated plain looked smiling and happy. We noticed how much farther advanced the wheat was here than in Shiraz; and yet Firuzabad is only 225 feet lower than Shiraz, and one degree farther south.

Firuzabad.

Zaki Beg, flagellating his ancient and hoary charger, rode on in advance, and told the Ilkhani of our coming. Quarters were assigned us in a new house within a newly-planted garden. I had an upper room, elegantly painted and carpeted. It was fourteen feet square by nine feet high, and one side was taken up by a large window constructed of small panes of red and yellow and blue and green glass. The Ilkhani soon came to see me. But he and his dominions deserve a separate chapter.

CHAPTER V.

FIRUZABAD.

12TH TO 14TH MARCH.

SULTAN MUHAMMAD, Ilkhani of Firuzabad, ought to be the head of the Iliat or nomad tribes of this district, as his father was before him. But in Persia more than elsewhere it is a misfortune to be "left an early orphan, and a selfish uncle's[1] ward;" and the headship of the clan has passed to Sultan Muhammad's first cousin, Dârâb Khan, who seems to be a kind of brigand on a magnificent scale. There remains, however, the title of Ilkhani, and the hereditary domain of Firuzabad, a fair property to any one who knows how to manage it. The plain is well-watered, and bears rich wheat and famous rice. It had thirty villages as many years ago,

---

[1] The Ilkhani's uncle is the redoubtable Qavvâm, whose sister is the Ilkhani's mother. The Qavvâm appropriated most of the personal property of his deceased brother-in-law.

but neglect and misgovernment have reduced their number to thirteen. The fault does not lie with the Ilkhani, who has been doing his best, since attaining his majority, for the improvement of his property; but in Persia villages are easily ruined, and restored with difficulty. Firuzabad suffered severely in last year's drought, when the river on which the plain depends for water became a bed of gravel and dust. Meanwhile, the Ilkhani has still some relics of his father's fortune, and entertains a chance European guest in the most splendid style of Oriental hospitality. Hardly had I unfolded my humble camp-chair upon the carpets of the room set apart for me, when servants came bearing trays with apparatus of sherbet and tea, the like of which I had never seen before. Gravely did the tea-maker spread before him a Persian rug, and place upon it in seemly order the bright *samovar*, the silver saucers, and the gay china cups. With like solemnity were the bowls of sherbet, the vases of lemon-water and rosewater, and the baskets of ice, arranged by the functionary in charge of that department. The whole presented a pleasing array of bright colours neatly disposed.

After refreshment, the Ilkhani was announced. He is a man of about thirty years, with a handsome face and very pleasant manners. A look of dreamy melancholy gives his face an interesting expression rare in Oriental physiognomy. He is fond of talking politics, and certainly seemed to be a well-wisher of the English; yet I found that he had by no means that adequate notion of the might of England which one would desire to see among educated Persians. " Why are you leaving Candahar ?" he asked. I explained that the country was not worth holding (the moral argument, that we had no right to be there, would not have been understood by a Persian). He accorded a polite assent, but plainly believed the true reason to be our incapacity to retain our conquest.

" Could you fight Russia ?" he asked next.

" Yes, of course we could."

" I doubt it. You might, if France or Prussia helped you, but not alone. How many soldiers have you, and how many soldiers has Russia ?"

The enumeration of the respective military forces confirmed the Ilkhani's opinion. I referred to the Crimean war and its battles.

" The Crimean war (*jang-i-Sistapul*) ? You did nothing. You were four to one, and you effected nothing at all."

Another point on which I could not get correct ideas into his head was British rule in India. I have seen many similar instances of educated Persians who evidently disbelieved the universal and paramount nature of our rule in India. One of the Ilkhani's attendants asked whether the native Princes were friendly towards Russia. The Ilkhani himself was firmly persuaded that we exacted a tribute from India. Perhaps, in a sense, he was not far wrong. In our second interview, next day, the Ilkhani again showed himself much impressed with the power and greatness of Russia. Having no fear of Russia myself, I listened with some amusement. Next day the Ilkhani invited Sayyid Ali to dinner. Knowing Sayyid Ali to be a genuine admirer of British rule in India, and extremely fond of narrating to a Persian audience the wonders which it has wrought in that country, I expected an account of the entertainment with some curiosity. It turned out that the Ilkhani, while the wine went round, bitterly upbraided the English for their lamentable supineness and indifference to their interests in Persia; the country had been allowed to sink under Russian influence; nevertheless, the English might annex Shiraz to-morrow, if they had only the spirit; they would be welcomed by the inhabitants; and so on.

I have dwelt so long on the Ilkhani's opinions because they are those of an educated Persian, of more than average intelligence, living in a part of the country which one would suppose more accessible to English influence than Russian.

The day after my arrival in Firuzabad had been wet, but on the following morning I was able to visit the ruins of old Firuzabad and the fire-temple. The Ilkhani's carriage took me to the old city, about four miles north of the modern town. We entered the walls through a gap where a gate had been. The wall and ditch can be traced distinctly, a circle of grass-grown mounds with a diameter of about three quarters of a mile. Inside are ruins of small stone-built houses, and in the centre a minar or *solid* stone pillar, twelve feet square, and fifty feet high. It had a staircase running round it outside, which was practicable till within the last ten years or so, but has mostly fallen away now. The tower is built of unhewn stone. Near it are the remains of a platform of hewn stone, and of two deep tanks once faced with stone. One tank is twenty feet deep; the size of the stones is four feet by two by two, and the material apparently white freestone. Both the city and the fire-temple are ascribed by tradition to Gushtasp, one of the earliest heroes of Persian romance. The Firuzabad river, which we had tracked from its source in the Dasht-i-Muak, after penetrating the northern mountains by the gorge I was unable to enter, crosses the plain, and makes its exit through the southern mountain-wall by a gorge of more majestic dimensions. Alexander the Great (so the legend says) built a dam at the mouth of this latter gorge, and the pent-up water flooded the plain, and destroyed the old city of Firuzabad. The holes in the rock are still to be seen at the mouth of the gorge, where Alexander fixed the iron spikes or clamps that held his dam together. In a later generation Firuz Shah broke the dam, drained the plain, and founded the modern town, called after his own name. It may have 4000 inhabitants.

The fire-temple, which stands high, had escaped the flood, but met its doom from Muhammad. When the prophet was born, the sacred fire went out, and in its place arose a spring of water, which may be seen to this day. We went to the spot. The temple stands close by the mouth of the northern gorge, where the river debouches on the plain. It is a strange building, in good preservation, though every year nibbles away a bit of it. Like the tower, it is built of unhewn stone, and very solidly; the walls are at least ten feet thick. Three domes, thirty feet in diameter and forty feet in height, formed the body of the temple. One wing consisted of a courtyard with covered buildings and passages; the other of lofty vaulted halls, the antechambers of the shrine. Two of the principal domes are entire, save for small gaps, and rents near the top; the third has half fallen; and the domed or vaulted roofs of the antechambers, which were not less than thirty feet high, have entirely disappeared. The walls are pierced by a gallery running round the central domes half-way up. It is impossible for a casual visitor to conjecture the meaning and purpose of these and other strange narrow passages that lead to nothing, or of the vaults which extend under the temple. I thought of the Guebres and their sun-worship, and looked towards the east; but the building faces no one cardinal point of the compass, being irregularly built north-east and south-west. A rough plan is subjoined.

Firuzabad.

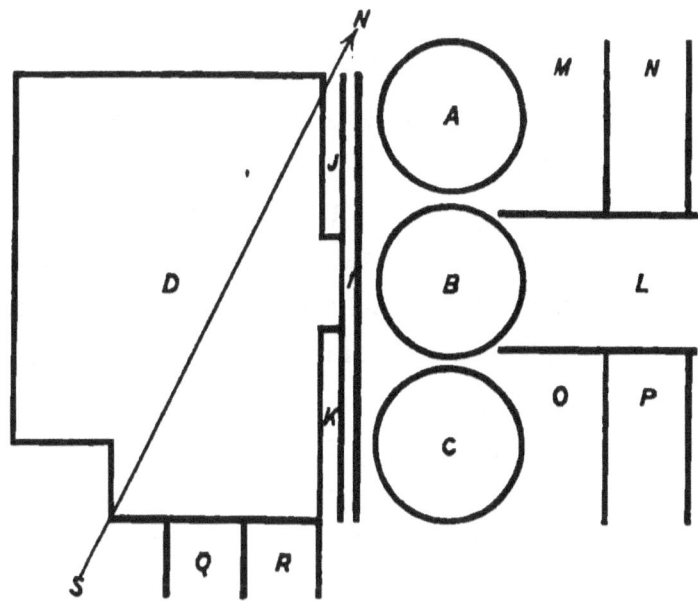

A, B, C, three domed chambers. Half the dome of C has fallen in.

D, the courtyard; it was divided into several rooms, probably roofed.

I, J, K, passages between courtyard and domes.

L, M, N, O, P, antechambers (*aiwan*); they had vaulted roofs, now fallen in.

Q, R, chambers outside the wall of the courtyard; these also had vaulted roofs.

From east to west the building and courtyard are about sixty yards wide. The rooms under the domes are square, with a side of about thirty feet. Part of the old plaster, one and a half inches thick, is still adhering to the walls. The domes and their adjoining chambers intercommunicate by doors.

East of the temple is the spring which gets credit for having been the original shrine of the sacred fire (âtash-kadah). It is a beautiful blue pool, and sends out a stream strong enough to turn a mill. In summer, when the water is low, the facing of a well can be seen at the bottom of the pool, and evidently the well was the reason why the temple was built there. A profusion of myrtle-bushes surrounds the spring.

Having viewed the temple I went into the mouth of the gorge, and saw some of the rock-carvings. Three knights in armour are tilting at full gallop; one has struck his adversary through the chest, the other through the head; the third seems to be pursuing a flying foe, well-nigh withdrawn from his rage by the saving (or destroying) hand of Time. Each victorious warrior bears that strange globular crest upon his helm which one notices on the carven kings of Persepolis. The figures are gigantic, and most spiritedly executed. Remains of an old causeway and staircase leading to them could be traced along the face of the cliff. There are other carvings higher up the gorge, but I had no time to visit them.

During my three days' stay in Firuzabad, I and my people were guests of the Ilkhani. On our departure he gave us a sack of Firuzabad rice, bread, oil, dates, and some bottles of wine for myself. I shall always have a kindly remembrance of his hospitality and courtesy. All I had to give in return were two small bowls of Moradabad metal-work.

96   *Six Months in Persia.*

CHAPTER VI.

FIRUZABAD TO LAR.

FORTY-NINE FARSAKHS; NINE DAYS.

I WAS nearly detained one day more in Firuzabad. The Ilkhani and Sayyid Ali celebrated the last night with festivities; nobody was up at six o'clock in the morning, and it was not till ten that the caravan got under way. Here it may be observed that the traveller in Persia must get up first and wake all his people, if he wishes to start early. Persian servants are in no wise to be trusted in this respect; indeed, they are next to worthless in all respects, but of this more anon. Between Bushire and Shiraz the *réveillé* used to be sounded by the Rev. Mr. Bruce; through the rest of my travels I had to do it for myself, and gradually grew accustomed to the operation.

15*th March, Kashkai tents,* 7 *farsakhs;* 10 *a.m. to* 6 *p.m.*—Bidding good-bye to the Ilk-

Tihdasht.

hani with many friendly expressions on both sides, we marched to the south-eastern end of the Firuzabad plain. "The plain was grassy, wild, and bare," five miles wide, with a rocky mountain-ridge on either hand. That on the left, rising 1500 to 2000 feet, was split here and there by great gaps running parallel to the summit, as if in prehistoric ages the redhot mass had broken in cooling, and the lower portion had sunk down, leaving a long crevasse with sheer sides 250 feet deep. These crevasses were dark in shadow, while the rest of the hill, in colour a light yellowish brown, seemed to reflect the bright sunlight. The eye travelled up the lighted slope, met the intense and brilliant blue of the sky above, and returned dazzled to the duller tints of the plain, half-green, half-brown. At eight miles from Firuzabad, we came to a small village called Tihdasht (the foot of the plain), situated immediately under the mountain, and backed by semicircular galleries of tabular rock—a natural amphitheatre of stone. Ruins of two other villages lie in the plain below. Tihdasht is built of stone, in an exceedingly dirty and narrow style of architecture. I asked an old inhabitant why such a situation had been chosen, against the southward-facing wall of rock, which must glow like an oven in summer. "God," said he, "has assigned us this place wherein to live."

Four miles further on we turned more southward, left the mountain range behind, and entered a broken region of little hills. On our right we caught a glimpse of the river, six miles distant; its course ran parallel to ours for a few miles, and then, turning abruptly southwards, it was lost in the huge mouth of a ravine which pierces the dark and lofty range that bounds this region on the south. This is the fifth mountain-cleft through which the adventurous river forces its way, and it is much the grandest of all. We could see the cliffs, 500 feet high, at its mouth, and could trace the zigzag windings of the cleft in the face of the mountain. A road crosses the mountain and meets the river again in the plain of Babonej. I might have marched that way, but had preferred our present route, as passing through an unknown country.

We were in search of an *ahshâm*[1] or encampment of the Nafar tribe of Kashkai Turks,

---

[1] The word is the plural of the Arabic *hashm*. It is used in Central and Southern Persia. I never heard the Turkoman word *yurt* till I reached Tcheran.

whose flocks graze in this hilly region during the early spring. It was quite uncertain where we should find them. About two o'clock we halted for lunch in a grassy hollow, gay with wild flowers. Some miles farther on we fell in with grazing cows and random patches of cultivation; and at last, near sunset, we discovered the welcome tents. They were black blankets stretched over four sticks. Half a dozen families were thus encamped on a level space above a small stream. Their headman received us kindly, spread a carpet for me, and surrounded it with a fence of matting, as they had no spare tent. After sunset the goats and sheep came home, pouring noisily over the low hills, amid much barking of dogs. The stars came out, the household fire was kindled before each tent, and from a little distance came the tinkle of the mule-bells, and the whinnying of the mules over their barley. Below us was the murmur of the stream; above, and on the left hand, high mountain-ridges showed dark against the deep blue with its stars. I drew a waterproof sheet over the edge of my enclosure, to make me a kind of tent. In the morning it was covered thickly with hoarfrost.

These nomads own allegiance to Darab Khan,

then in Bibahan with the bulk of his tribe, in the train of the Ihtisham. They pay him revenue in the shape of a poll-tax on cattle, and he pays the provincial governor. Like most of the Persian nomad tribes, they have their winter and summer quarters (*qishláq* and *iláq*); the latter are among the high mountains west of the Shiraz and Isfahan road, and are visited from the end of spring to the end of autumn. Soon after the *nauruz* or first day of the Persian astronomical year—the time when

The yonge sonne
Hath in the Lambe his halfe course yronne—

the Kashkais begin their march towards the cool altitudes of snow-clad Pâdinâ. They leave some men behind them to reap the scattered fields which they have ploughed and sown in their Firuzabad *qishláq* or winter haunts. The grain is buried in pits against the return of the tribe next winter. They spoke well of Darab Khan, as being a better administrator than the Ilkhani. It is possible; the latter is perhaps too refined for a leader of nomads. Darab Khan got his appointment five years ago.

16*th March, Shaludan,* 7 *farsakhs;* 8 *a.m. to* 6 *p.m.*—We started early next morning, and marched four miles among the tangled low

A Valley of Flowers.

hills to an ascent of 200 feet, which lifted us into a narrow plain. After five miles more this sank into a network of ravines, all dry, and paved with white stones that dazzled the eye under the bright sunlight. Wandering up and down and along these, we came by one o'clock on the source of a stream, and halted for lunch on its banks. The sun was hot, but the water restored freshness to man and beast. Our route followed the stream. Gradually the minor ravines disappeared, and the confused tangle of heights and hollows shaped itself into a valley, which grew narrower as we advanced. On the left was a steep wall of rock, 500 feet high (they call it the black wing, *par-i-siyah*); on the right, precipitous headlands alternated with level bays of verdure and flowers. At last the valley narrowed to 400 yards, and we were marching in the meadows beside the stream, where the grass was knee-deep, and the clover ankle-deep, and flowers grew in profusion—daisies, dandelions, small celandine, marsh-mallows, scarlet poppies, vetches, veronica, blue and white hyacinths, nightstock, yellow mustard-flower, the white bells of the camel-thorn, and the blue stars which are slandered by the name of squills. I had never seen such a land of flowers. Late in the afternoon we passed the village fort of Raikân high on the left; then we dipped into the bed of the stream, through marshy ground and willows, and tall reeds; finally, we caught a welcome glimpse of a small fort, showing white against a green brae, and knew it for Shaludun, our halting-place for the night.

Wild rhubarb grew plentifully under the cliffs on the right bank of the stream. I gathered some, but it proved bitter and useless. Sayyid Ali stayed behind to collect more, lost his way, and did not come in till after dark. Meanwhile we alighted at the door of the little fort, and asked for shelter. An inspection of the interior tended to confirm the kadkhuda's assurances that the place swarmed with fleas. We decided to camp on a level space outside, where a black tent was pitched for me. I ran down to the stream, and had a glorious bathe. A cuckoo began to call as the setting sun threw his rays against the western wall of rock. As the daylight died, the tiny valley seemed more than ever remote and secluded from the world.

Shaludun means "rice-holding," and there was in fact a good deal of rice in terrace fields along the stream. A good garden of lemons lay behind the fort; it belongs to the landlord, an Arab Sayyid in the service of the heir apparent, then governing (or misgoverning) Azarbaijan. The Sayyid was accustomed to have the lemons converted into lemon-juice, bottled in Kîr, and sent to Tabriz for his august master. As for the tenants, with whom I had a friendly chat round a fire after dinner, the narrow circumstances of the village do not afford much scope for improvement. The eight families who inhabit the fort know little of the world beyond their own valley, where they maintain a squalid struggle for existence. Still, they were well nourished, and fairly well clad, and the fields showed traces of labour and ingenuity. We talked of the heat of summer, which must be pretty severe in this valley, but the people assured me that they preferred the summer, and would rather bear heat than cold. I remember receiving the same answer from a field labourer in the north-western provinces of India. "Are there any melons grown here?" I asked. "O yes," said the kadkhuda, "we have some asses and goats." He had mistaken *khar-buza* (a melon) for *khar* and *buz* (an ass and a goat), and so answered beside the point, and gave us all a laugh. The kadkhuda was an elderly man, but had never been so far as Shiraz. He told a story of some man of Shaludun who made that long journey years ago. On his return, a fellow-villager asked him whether in Shiraz he had not said his prayers (*namáz khwándíd*). "Certainly," he replied, mistaking *khwándíd* (recited) for *khurdíd* (ate), "I ate *namaz* and many other gook things in Shiraz." He did not know the meaning of the word *namaz*, prayers; and most of the Shaludun folk, I was assured, were unable to say their prayers, though they have a little mud-built saint's shrine under the village, where they celebrate religious observances of some sort. Yet for all their ignorance, these remote rustics knew (what struck me greatly) the names both of Russia and England. Had the Russians, they asked, lately captured a strong place in the north? This looked like rumours of the second Turkoman campaign. From curiosity, I asked them which they thought the greater, Russia or England? "England," said the Kadkhuda, "was a small thing (*chizi kuchak*), of which they had heard; but Russia was always known, and famous, and bigger and stronger." In the midst of this high political discourse, suddenly a man in the corner broke silence. "*Our* city," said he, "*our* city is Kir." This was the signal for universal hearty laughter, it came in so absurdly. We saw enough of the "city" of Kir next day.

17th March, Kir, 5 *farsakhs;* 8 *a.m.* to 3 *p.m.*—Hitherto we had been marching south-eastwards, but Kir is nearly south of Shaludun, and behind a range of mountains. The first half of the road runs up a long strath in the hills, ending in a saddle-back over which is nothing but blue sky. The richness and beauty of the mountain slopes were admirable.

> The lawns and meadow-ledges half-way down
> Hung rich in flowers.

And such plenty and perfection, too, of grass and clover, and all manner of herbage—and the almond-trees were in full bloom, like the blossoming hawthorn [2] on an Irish hill-side. Whole beds and bands of yellow, and blue, and blazing scarlet, shone along the foot or up the slopes of the hills. Far away, on our left front, the high

---

[2] "And the almond-tree shall flourish." One understands that text after travelling in these parts of Persia, where the almond-bushes are hoary with bloom in the spring.

dark mountains of Jahrum rose against the horizon. Over all shone—one might almost say sparkled—the marvellous brilliancy of the Persian sky. At last we reached the saddleback, and saw before us a steep and narrow pass between high walls of rock, and at the bottom a glimpse of green fields, a corner of the plain of Kir. We were an hour and a half in descending to an *abambar* or roofed cistern of water, in a little meadow, where we held our noonday halt. Thence the downward road winds round the sides and spurs of the hills, coming out finally on a long rocky slope which has been the scene of a miracle. Ali rode over it on his horse Duldul, and the hoofmarks of Duldul can be seen in the solid rock to this day. Most of them are reverentially surrounded with circles of small stones. The wells of a *qanat* are also to be traced in orderly succession along the rocky expanse, and probably the hoofmarks have some connexion with them, and were useful in marking distances. Apart from these memorials, the bare slope of brown rock itself is worth seeing. Rock takes strange forms in Persia, whether massed into mountains or broken into cliffs, or ranged in broad shelves, or set on end like a huge wall of masonry, or recumbent and traversable as it is here. The qanat is of unknown antiquity, yet perhaps it works still; at least, a spring breaks out at the foot of the slope, and helps to water Kir. We rode along the water-channel, in the warm afternoon air, through flowery meadows, past a little marsh with tall yellow iris, between fields where the young corn was already high, and under the walls of gardens thick with orange-trees and pomegranate. Women were bathing in the streamlet; one, quite naked, turned her back to us and regarded us not. Men met me on the road, looked at the strange figure, and gave friendly greeting. We entered Kir, and found it a large village, much in ruin, with three or four poor shops. The ruler of the district was absent, nobody had been left in his place, and we sought quarters in the caravan-sarai, where I immediately became the centre of an inquisitive crowd of traders, camel-drivers, and loafers of the street.

I got a pretty fair upper room, with doors. The kadkhuda came to see me before long—a tall, red-bearded man, with a squint. After talk about revenue matters, he professed himself anxious to ask my advice. He has a date-grove; it was planted by his father, but the governor of the district takes the dates. Appeal to Shiraz is useless; the Mutamid is bribed, and will not grant redress. He thought of going to Teheran with his complaint, but the governor stopped him. I gave him my sympathy, and could do no more. But why was I travelling about the country? This, as I often found, was a point on which the Persian mind refused to be enlightened. To a Persian it is incredible that any man can be such a fool as to waste his money in searching for information on geographical and revenue matters; he must be paid for his trouble by somebody; he must have some deep purpose of making money by the business. After sunset I went out, and became the centre of a crowd. They complained that they were hungry, that it was impossible to earn one's living; and asked whether there were beggars in Europe (*Farang*). The fact was, I had now reached the edge of the famine tract. Among the crowd I found a man who had heard of Bombay, but nobody knew of England, nor had ever seen an Englishman. Some of them talked Turki.

The plain of Kir is about twenty-five miles long, and lies nearly east and west. It is said to contain thirty villages. Most of it is watered from the Qara-Agach. It is fertile when the water is in sufficient quantity, and produces corn as tall as a man. So, at least, said the kadkhuda. He asked me, by the way, whether the Sultan had any quarrel with Persia (*Sultan i Rum bá Iran harfi dárad*), referring evidently to the Kurdish invasion, and the encouragement of the Kurd Obaidullah by the Turkish authorities.

An earthen fort stands in the plain above the town. In the reign of Muhammad Shah (before 1852) it was held by 200 men against the father of the Ilkhani of Firuzabad, who besieged it with 10,000 horse (*sic*) and two guns. The owner of the fort was outside, and communicated with the garrison, with a view to raising the siege. One of his letters was intercepted, and he and his followers were waylaid by a superior force. He cut his way through, and fled to a mud fort, but was soon starved out, and, with thirteen of his people, was paraded in chains in sight of the Kir garrison, and put to death. The garrison, however, held out, and the Ilkhani being evidently useless, a Jahrum man was commissioned to try his luck, who succeeded in making terms, let the garrison depart in peace, and then dismantled the fort, which has never since been repaired. Persia has made some progress since those days. Such difficulties could hardly arise now.

An amirzada, or Persian nobleman, who had recently passed through Kir, did me an unintentional disservice by feasting all the beggars in the place, that is, three-fourths of the population. He had a thirty-*man*[3] pilau prepared, that is, two hundredweight of rice and flesh, and afterwards threw twenty-five tomans in copper among the crowd, by way of largess. In return, he was furnished with a guide who undertook to take him to Firuzabad in one day, across the mountains, the result being that the whole party were belated in the wilderness, and spent the night in much discomfort. At the door of the caravansarai, as we were starting, Sayyid Ali paid some trifling rewards for attendance. Forthwith he was surrounded by a crowd of beggars, who pressed on him and went near to snatch the purse out of his hand. I, safe on horseback, watched his face growing rapidly longer. Pulling out a handful of coppers, he threw them over the heads of the

[3] The Tabriz *man* is equivalent to about $6\frac{1}{2}$ lbs. The *shahman*, which is the Isfahan standard of weight, is twice as heavy.

crowd; the beggars turned on the spoil, and Sayyid Ali nimbly mounted his charger.

18th March, Sargah, 10 *farsakhs;* 7.30 *a.m.* *to* 9 *p.m.*—We had now descended into a warmer region, where date-palms and cactus betrayed a semi-tropical climate. The nearest regular stage was Harm, nearly fifty miles distant, but our guide proposed that we should camp by a pool in the wilderness, and reach Harm next day. The road runs behind low hills bordering the Kir plain on its right or southern side, and proceeds nearly due east for twelve miles, till it comes down on the Qara-Agach, here flowing in a southerly direction. A very quaint old bridge crosses the river. It is called the Bride's Bridge (*pul i arûs*), but nobody seems to know who built its high stone-arches, laid the zigzag roadway across them, and constructed the towers and vaulted rooms in its piers. It is the queerest structure, in the way of a bridge, that I ever saw in picture or reality; it is zigzag in shape, and two storied, the roadway being in the second story. The Qara-Agach flows between high banks, with a strong turbid stream sixty yards broad; the centre of the bridge stands fully forty feet above the stream, yet the floodmark is half way up the piers.

We now entered broken country with low rocky hills, which gradually sank into a long plain, sloping to the south-east, enclosed between two low rocky ranges three miles apart, and covered with wild oats and thin grass, shot through with flowers. For all its greenness this desert was perfectly waterless, save a few holes which the winter rain had filled. At the outset we passed some of these of considerable size, with bushes and cactus shrubs near the water, reminding me of Indian scenery; but the water was brackish. We passed also a party of Kashkai[1] Turks, reclining under the shade of *kunar* bushes, beside an old brick tank. These Turks were bound for Bidshahr with revenue for the governor Lutf Ali Khan. An hour and a half later, as we were halted for breakfast near a pool, the Turks came up, and proposed that we should ride with them to their tents, which were represented as a few farsakhs distant. We went together over the green but arid plain, which seemed endless. The day was hot, and we vainly turned aside to the ruins of various old stone cisterns, in

---

[1] Kashkai means *profugi*, from the Turki *qáchmaq*, to flee. The ancestors of the tribe took refuge in Persia centuries ago.

Antelope-shooting.

the hope of water which was not there. Flies were abundant, and troubled the horses. It was not till two hours before sunset that we reached a water-hole, with muddy water, full of tadpoles. Sayyid Ali had ridden on in advance, with the principal Turk. His stoutness made him feel the heat more than another, and I found him reclining under a bush in a state of thankfulness for deliverance from death by thirst. We drank freely of the muddy pool, and having smoked the necessary *qalyan*, and seen the mules arrive, we set out again in search of the Kashkai tents. The plain ended in a pass between low rocky hills. Some antelopes were seen in one of the recesses of the plain between the hills on our right. Off went three of the Turks at full gallop over the stony ground; presently we heard two shots, and in half an hour the chief man rejoined us with a dead antelope slung under his horse's belly. Persians are accustomed to shoot from horseback, and to ride at full speed over the worst ground.

This diversion beguiled the way a little. From the low pass we looked down upon a green plain, with a large sheet of shallow water in the middle. In the descent, one of the Turks took to singing selections from the Shahnama, in a lamentable voice. The praises of Rustam are dear to the Persian heart, and my Kashkai chanted with great gusto the hero's words to the prince whom he had loyally fought for and crowned.

> *Agar man paziraftami taj o takht,*
> *Na budi tura in buzurgi o rakht.*

"Had *I* accepted the crown and throne, *thou* wouldst have had none of this greatness and pomp."

Meanwhile, daylight died, and no tents were visible. The Turks had a mare running loose; she disappeared ahead in the darkness, seeking the camp, and the Turks rode after her, bidding us wait their return. Left alone, we took the advice of our guide, and turned aside to a village at the foot of the hills on our left. It was dark when we reached the walls and found the place deserted—a date-grove with ruined houses. A heavy dew was falling, the mules were wading knee-deep in the luxuriant vegetation of the plain, we had no fuel, and could find no water. All the air was faint with the odour of the night-stock (*shab-bu* or night-blowing ceres) which grew thick among the grass. Our guide was confident of the existence of a village, and after casting about, he lighted on a path which took us to a small village fort. Through the open door we could see the light of a fire burning in the courtyard. Suddenly the light went out; the inhabitants had heard us coming, and shut the door against possible robbers. In vain did we knock and expostulate; we were received at first by silence, and then by advice to go elsewhere. There was no other village within six miles, and we could not find our way in the dark. The situation was ludicrous enough, and the energetic eloquence of Sayyid Ali heightened its absurdity. "We have come from his Highness the Governor of Shiraz," cried he, in an elevated tone of voice, "and bear written orders from him, which you will disobey at your peril. We have a ghulam of his Highness with us, who possesses a tongue, though you mightn't think it, for he doesn't choose to use it, apparently" (this by way of reproof to poor old Zaki Beg, who stood by, holding his ancient steed, quite flabbergasted). "You are afraid of robbers, are you? Have the goodness to get up on the wall, and look at us. Do we look like robbers? Pray observe the laden mules. See the Sahib himself, one of the grandees of Farangistan, whom you had better treat with due respect, or it will be the worse for you." Presently a man with a long gun appeared on the wall, and provoked a general chorus of muleteers, servants, and all; but the garrison showed little sign of yielding. Then it occurred to me to step forward and try my persuasive powers. "Contemplate me," I said; "I am a Farangi, and no robber. See the fashion of my clothes; this also is my hat" (waving a huge white pith hat, which glimmered ghostly in the starlight). The hat carried conviction with it, and the door was unbarred. The mules, poor beasts, were glad to be unloaded after their march of forty miles; and we all welcomed the shelter of the fort, poor as it was. I spread my bed in a niche of the gateway, frequented by early-rising cows.

They call this place Sargah. It has suffered much from robbers of late years. The delay in admitting us was excused by the fact that some time before, a robber had got in on pretence of being a Government servant with his retinue, and had walked off with their cattle. Sargah has also been short of water for the last four years. It has now been bought by a man of substance, who has repaired the qanat on which the village depends.

We had been in the fort half an hour, when the Turks came in, profuse in apologies for having left us. They wanted me to visit their tents next day. They were not bad fellows, but profoundly ignorant of the existence of England or India. Talking about their summer-quarters, the chief man assured me that a Russian officer (Urusti) had come among them last summer, and won admiration by his straight shooting and his powers of endurance as a mountaineer. Now, this Russian was no other man than Captain Durand, assistant political agent at Bushire. I thought it a strange testimony to the familiarity of the Russian name, that an English officer should actually be mistaken for a Russian by people among whom he had lived for some weeks. I myself was taken for a Russian by the street-boys of Isfahan.

19th March, Karyun, 2 farsakhs. — Next morning we marched five miles to Harm, and three miles more to Karyun. We crossed a muddy part of the plain, by the borders of the shallow water, where a few egrets were standing, and some terns were flying overhead. The air was hot and moist, the plain luxuriantly green with grass and herbage, and wild oats. Nothing I ever saw in Persia reminded me so strongly of India. Unfortunately there were other points of resemblance. I had seen a famine in India; I was now, for many days, to see the effects of drought and famine in Persia. Harm is a large village, with extensive date-groves, and perhaps two hundred houses. It was deserted and in ruins; we could find no quarters there. Karyun is still larger; it must have had a population of 2000 souls, but we could find only three families in the whole place. We rode about nearly half an hour, vainly seeking an inhabitant who might guide us to a house. Sayyid Ali was for putting up in a mosque, but I thought the *mihmankhana* or public rest-house, though ruined, would suit us better. I got a fair upper room, without doors, and quarters were found below for all my people.

We were now within the district of Lutf Ali Khan, of Bidshahr, the revenue-farmer and governor of Bidshahr and Harm, with their dependencies. His tufangchis refused us admission into the mud fort outside Karyun, on the ground that Lutf Ali's harem was there. Two other forts stand in the plain, a mile east of Karyun. One is the Mud Fort (*Qala-i-Gili*), built when Karim Khan was reigning in Shiraz (1780); it is a square earthwork with a side of 120 yards, and had a tower every twelve yards. The other is the fort of the Fire-well, so called from the discovery of naphtha in a well hard by; it is a tower girt with a wall, on a mound. Forts and well are in ruins now. Karyun stands in the middle of three rocky hills, and these, also, are said to have been fortified. I went up one hill with some men of the village. They stopped at the foot, picked up bones, and said, "These are bones of men," and proceeded to tell me the following story:— Shah Kâran was besieged here by 12,000 Mussalmans, when the Arabs first invaded Persia. While they were at their prayers he sallied out. They would not leave their prayers, and he slew them all without resistance. In the Mussalman camp were forty virgins, who thus fell into the hands of Shah Kâran. These young women, being of virtuous principles, besought deliverance from Heaven, and accordingly the earth opened and swallowed them all up—except three who fled, with Shah Kâran and his men after them. One maiden ran across the plain, and up the northern mountains, and was now on the point of capture, when a cave disclosed itself in the mountain-side; she ran in, and was lost. The cave is called the Ghar Bibi, or Lady's Cave, to this day, and is well known to have no end. The second maiden fled to the mountains of Khunj, far to the south, and died there of exhaustion. Her shrine, called that of the Bibi darmânda, or Tired-out Lady, is a famous place of prayer for childless wives. The third maiden disappeared in some other mountain-side, and water has trickled from the cleft ever since.

Word of this catastrophe was brought to Hâjat, who had conquered Kir. He came over with an army to avenge his brother, but could not take the fort. At last Shah Kâran's wife cast eye upon Hâjat, and fell in love with him. He promised to marry her if she would betray the fort. She endeavoured, Delilah-like, to wheedle her husband out of the magic secret which made him unconquerable. He, too, like Samson, seems to have had a plentiful crop of hair, not, however, confined to his head only. He bade her cut hair from his breast, and bind his thumbs and great toes together with it. She did so, and cried, "The Mussalmans be upon thee, Shah Kâran." But he broke his bonds, and the assault failed. Further coaxing persuaded him to tell her that she ought to have poured water on the fastenings, and when she had tied him up again and done so, his strength and soldiership departed, and the fort was taken. Hâjat married Shah Kâran's wife, and immediately cut off her head, remarking that he didn't wish her to betray *him*, too, on some future occasion. He then began to search for Shah Kâran's buried treasure. Being divinely (or diabolically) informed that the way to find it was to cause blood to flow down the hill-side like water, he conducted the population of Karyun to the top of the hill, and there proceeded to cut their throats. This went on several days, without revealing any treasure, till it came to the turn of an old woman and her two sons. The old woman offered to show Hâjat a better way. "In the vaults," she said, "there is great store of wine, the blood of the grape. Pour *that* over the rocks, and you will find the treasure without all this blood-guiltiness." Hâjat did so; and when the last jar of wine was removed, the door of the treasure-house appeared behind it.

Such, condensed, is the legend of Karyun. Shah Kâran was, of course, a fire-worshipper,[5] and seems to be a semi-historical personage. He is credited with having made sixty qanats.

[5] The Chah Tashi (*atashi*) or fire-well, was perhaps a holy place in Shah Qaran's time.

It is probable enough, too, that Karyun may be an ancient place. In a country like Persia, where the habitable spots have been marked out by Nature from the beginning of the world, the smallest human settlement in the desert may date back thousands of years. It is at least true of Karyun that the ruins of a fort do actually stand on the hill, and that bones are plentiful in the dry torrent beds.

What with relics of mortality, ruins, and robbers, Karyun was an eminently cheerful place. From the hill-top one looked down on the ruins of the village. My guides said there were twenty inhabited houses; I doubt it. The place was once flourishing and well-built. Conical domes of *abambars* (water-cisterns) rose among the houses, testifying to a large water-supply and a large population in former years. My guides complained much of robbers, and of the misgovernment of the Qajars, i.e. the present royal family. The day before my arrival a band of robbers had sacked a village of Bidshahr. Karyun itself had been desolate these twenty years, so they said, but their complaints were exaggerated. Of supposed insecurity of property, I had, however, some proofs. The herdsmen on the hills were armed with guns, and through the night I was awakened by the firing of armed watchmen in the streets—the oriental way of showing that one is on the alert.

Karyun and Harm are owned by Lutf Ali Khan, who also owned Sargah, but had to sell it to pay his debts. In good seasons, the plain where these villages (and a few others) are situated ought to be extremely rich. I saw some very fine wheat under Karyun. An ancient qanat waters Karyun, and an unsuccessful attempt has recently been made by Lutf Ali Khan to strike out another. But we were now sinking below the region of qanats, and entering that of cultivation dependent upon wells, or on the rain from heaven.

The most momentous event for me on this day, the 19th of March, was one which I omitted to chronicle, because I was not aware of it. It happened in the Antipodes.

20th March, Bidshahr, 6 farsakhs; 6.30 a.m. to 2.30 p.m.—Our march to Bidshahr[6] next day took us over the tops of low hills, covered with camel-thorn, which looked not unlike Irish bog and heather under the cloudy sky. Between

---

[6] "Willow-city." There are far more tamarisks than willows in the Bidshahr plain nowadays.

the hill-tops were little plains, and finally we climbed up a rocky pass, and saw the Bidshahr plain at our feet. It was wide and green, with groves of date-palms and clumps of tamarisks large as full-grown willow-trees. On our left the plain sank into a shallow salt lake. We were now entering the salt country. The water-holes which we passed on our march held brackish water. There were several abambars on the road; one of these held water, and we breakfasted beside it.

Under gentle rain we entered Bidshahr, and found it as large as Karyun, and nearly as desolate. Lutf Ali Khan's fort was a tumble-down mud edifice, and our quarters in the mihmankhana were not much better than those of the day before. We found our friends the Turks there; they were in light marching order, and had gained a day on us. They brought 225 tomans for Lutf Ali Khan, in silver, a queer mixture of coins, including old English crown-pieces and gigantic Spanish doubloons. Lutf Ali Khan came to see me, looked at my guns, and asked me if I was not afraid of robbers, and whether I should resist if they stopped me. He lamented the ruined state of the country, and desired to know why I was travelling. I told him the reason was, to see Persia; which he did not believe. At dinnertime the Turks came in and asked leave to see me eat; so I showed them the uses of a knife and fork.

Bidshahr plain has never had a qanat. Wells can be sunk anywhere, but the water is brackish. Good wheat is grown, but the most paying crop is tobacco, for which the saline soil is well adapted. The tobacco of Hirum, on the north-eastern border of the plain, beyond the salt lake, is famous as far as Teheran. Last year all the abambars (which are very numerous) ran dry, and the people had to drink well-water.

21st March, Kaura, one farsakh.—Next morning dawned inauspiciously with clouds and rain, and Sayyid Ali had fever. Lutf Ali Khan sent me over a good breakfast, and as the day cleared I determined to march four miles to Kaura, on the southern side of the plain. Lutf Ali was very anxious that I should give him my shot-gun, but that, of course, was out of the question. He was good enough to say that he had been much pleased with me; I bade him good-bye, and we reached Kaura in an hour. Finding no quarters in the fort outside the village (this fort is notable as having a ditch round it) we went to the house of a man whose father had been the chief person in Kaura. This worthy was sixty years old, had never seen a European before, and evidently was not quite easy in his mind as to my intentions. He became reassured after a little, and talked. His father had been in service in Tabriz, and having saved money, and purchased, no doubt, the farm of the revenues of Kaura, came to his native village, built a fort on the hill above it, and made himself comfortable. The grandfather of Lutf Ali Khan took his fort, killed him, and spoiled his goods. The son retained only part of the family lands, and these are passing from him. One could not expect a man with such a history to be enchanted with the present régime. "*Fars tamam shud,*" he said, " the province is done for; every one is at the mercy of his more powerful neighbour (*har ki zur-ash ba digari mirasad*). The revenue demand is excessive (*Diwan maliyat-i-ziyada migirad*), and the ryots have fled away." Yet it seems that this deplorable state of things has arisen only since the death of the old governor of Bidshahr, one Bakir (probably a friend of my host), eight years ago.

I went up the hill, visited the ruins of the fort, and got a good view over the plain. While there, we saw a rider with a couple of mules enter the village. This was an officer from Shiraz, sent to settle a dispute about tobacco. A merchant of Jahrum had bought 4000 *mans* of tobacco from the villages of Bidshahr; some of it turned out bad, and the ryots were now to replace it or return the price. I called on this officer, and desired him to present my respects to the prince on his return to Shiraz. He was a comparatively enlightened person, knew the name of England, and surprised me by asking whether we were at war with Russia. He remarked that Russia had become very powerful of late years (*ajab dastawezi paida karda ast*).

Kaura ought to have 500 inhabitants, but only ten houses were actually occupied. The wells were noticeable objects. They are worked, as in India, by bullocks driven down an inclined plane, which draw up a leather bucket by a rope passing over a pulley; but the whole contrivance is on a larger scale than in India, the uprights are pillars of mud supporting the axle of the pulley at a height of fifteen feet, and the sloping bullock-walk is longer and deeper. The water level is about forty feet from the surface.

22nd March, Iwaz, 5 farsakhs; 7 a.m. to 2 p.m. The night was so chilly that I called for a fire. Marching next morning at dawn, I found my hands slightly numb till after sunrise. The road entered a wide pass between the southeastern hills, and came out on a plain between low mountain-ranges. Since leaving Firuzabad, we had watched the mountains gradually decrease in height. They are all disposed in parallel ranges, running north-west and south-east, with low transverse spurs connecting them, and as one marches south-eastwards between two of these parallel ranges, and crosses the spurs into plain after plain, each lower than the last, one finds that the mountains too sink lower, till from the Pidanau and Aigar ranges, rising 2000 feet on the left hand and the right of the Firuzabad plain (itself 5000 feet above the sea), they sink into the Mahruzi and Darbast hills, scarce 600 feet high, enclosing a narrow plain perhaps 300 feet above the sea. The vegetation also changes. Mastich (*bana*) and almond-trees and wild olive give place to kunar and tamarisk, and gardens of plane-trees are changed for groves of date-palm. The flowers grow fewer;

in to-day's march we saw hardly anything but night-stock, which covered some of the low hills as with a pale purple carpet. As the hills sink, they become steeper, and in the first half of the march from Kaura to Iwaz they present a face of sheer black cliff 600 feet high at one point on the left.

In the plain which we had now entered stand the ruins of three villages, and one village with a tower and ten inhabited houses. The plain is cultivated in good seasons, but four years of drought had left the people no seed to sow after last winter's plentiful rains. Crossing dry salt hollows at the lower end of the plain, the road enters salt hills marked by the usual variety of form and colour—flat-topped, conical or round, light green, red or blue, grey or rich brown. We crossed a stream of limpid water, the bitterest I ever tasted, and halted by an abambar in a small level space, covered with rich grass and flowers, and surrounded by grey peaks. On one of these a ragged fellow appeared with a gun, and shouted. Zaki Beg, informing me that he had carefully loaded his gun with ball that morning, urged his white animal forward to reconnoitre. (I subsequently became acquainted with his style of loading;

the charge of powder might possibly propel the bullet twenty yards.) Two or three more men appeared, and they all turned out to be shepherds, anxious to know what we meant to do. We reasoned with them, but could not induce them to come near. Marching again, as we topped a hill, a caravan of donkeys appeared on the hill opposite, coming our way, and escorted by some tufangchis, whom the sight of us threw into momentary excitement. When we met, one of the drivers asked me with apparent anxiety whether I had heard of robbers in Bidshahr. I told him of the reported sack of a village a few days before.

Winding round hill after hill, we came at last to a low saddle-back, over which the fort and houses of Iwaz stood out white upon a narrow green plain. The houses looked taller and better than any we had seen for some days, and we got capital quarters in the hall of the kalantar's house. The village has a population of about 1000, though it is partly uninhabited. It is full of abambars, some of which are very large, with high-domed roofs of stone. The well-water is brackish. The kalantar told me of the sufferings of the people in last year's famine, after three years of insufficient rain. Many died, others wandered away, and the poor who remained were reduced to eating the ground shells of the wild almond (*ahluk*).

Among the crowd which gathered at the door to gaze on the Farangi, I saw two youths in semi-Indian dress. They were dealers in English printed goods, and had been to Bombay, where they had picked up much impudence and a very little Hindustani. They praised Bombay and the English Government, and wanted to sell me a horse. There are a few merchants' houses in Iwaz, and on the whole the place is comparatively flourishing.

The kalantar gave me a capital dinner, and informed me of recent events in Jahrum.[7] Six months ago the governor of that place had occasion to punish a *luti*, that is, a professional blackguard. The man's comrades laid wait for the governor, and shot him at the gate of a garden where he had been enjoying a picnic. For this the Mutamid ud Daulat sent orders from Shiraz that Jahrum should be levelled, and the plough passed over the site; but means were found to

---

[7] Jahrum lies seventy miles north of Iwaz, and seems to be an artistic city. Lutf Ali Khan's walls in Bidshahr are adorned with pictures in a bold style of design and colouring, the work of a man of Jahrum.

allay his fury. One of the murderers has been executed, and three are in prison in Shiraz.

23rd March, Lar, 6 farsakhs; 6.30 a.m. to 2 p.m.—The Iwaz plain is twenty miles long, and little more than a mile wide. We marched down it next day, and halted to breakfast near an old shrine surrounded by ruined abambars, and by kunar and tamarisk-trees. A larger shrine, in good repair, lifts its white dome above a thick grove of these trees, two miles further on, and appears glorious as an enchanted palace from afar to the traveller toiling over the hot and shelterless plain. We did not visit it, but turned to the right among limestone hills. Patches of wheat grew in their hollows, and a small watercourse betrayed the proximity of Lar. At length we passed between two hills, and discovered Lar on our right front. The hill on the right was fortified, or had been fortified; that on the left had a hermit's house built against its steep white side, near the summit.

We took up our quarters in the Bagh-i-Nishat, or Pleasant Garden, half a mile outside the city. The gardener's family, who were in charge of the garden-house, swept the rooms for us, and we made ourselves comfortable, sending Zaki Beg to give notice of my arrival to Fath Ali Khan, the Governor of Lar.

CHAPTER VII.

LAR.

23RD TO 25TH MARCH.

FATH ALI KHAN came to see me in the afternoon. He is a tall and powerfully-built man, with a black beard; a dignified and orthodox man, the very impersonation of all the gravity and straitness of Islam—seemly in person, decorous in apparel, stately in speech, courteous yet reserved in demeanour, and so religious that he fills up the intervals of conversation with pious ejaculations and the telling of beads. His dress was half Arab; he wore a large silk turban and an Arab cloak. With him came one Safa Ali, who called himself the Prophet of Thieves (*paighambar i duzdan*). I found out something about this worthy in the course of my travels. He seems to be a native of Mahun, near Karman, and to follow the trade of wit, poet, and panegyrist. The uncle of the Shah (the Hisam us Sultanat, or Sword of the

Empire, late Governor of Khurasan), who appears to have a liking for such people, took a great fancy to him, and was his patron for some time. How he came to Lar I could not exactly ascertain; but at any rate Fath Ali found his society so agreeable that Safa Ali could not get permission to go elsewhere. His wife came from Karman for him not long ago, and had to go back without him. The strange thing is that such a man as Fath Ali should tolerate the daring jests and loose tongue of the prophet of thieves, who does not scruple to mock at heaven and hell, and even to travesty the Koran.

Besides Safa Ali, the captain of the artillery corps of Lar accompanied Fath Ali Khan. He wore his uniform, and looked like the generality of military officers in Persia, an underpaid disappointed man.

Fath Ali's bigotry could not help showing itself through his studiously polite manner. He talked little, and for the most part about religion. Was I a Catholic or a Protestant? he asked, somewhat to my surprise. The prophet took up the running, and wanted to know whether I had any reverence for Mecca, and whether I believed in Omar, Abu Bakr, and the rest. Questions like these are occasionally put to the traveller in Persia, and are rather puzzling to answer. One does not wish to be rude; yet with all imaginable liberality in matters religious, it is impossible to say that one believes in the saintliness of these calamitous characters. Later on, I found, or thought I found, a way out of the difficulty; but in the present case I only said that Englishmen were taught to respect every one's religious belief, and that indeed the greatest Persian poet preached the same doctrine, for Hafiz had written,—

*Hama kas tálib i Yár and, cha hushyár o cha mast;
Har já khana i ishq ast, cha masjid cha kinisht.*

"All seek the Friend, be they drunk or sober; every place is the house of Love, be it mosque or tavern." He professed himself immensely struck with the aptness of this quotation. Next day Fath Ali asked me to come and see the marriage festivities of his son. I found the party sitting in a room adorned with mirrors, and with pictures taken from rolls of piece-goods, and set in the white plaster of the walls. The Persians can make capital stucco, hard and smooth as marble; and they frame pictures and mirrors in this, and cut out floral designs in it, often with great taste and beauty. The walls of the Bagh-i-Nishat are very handsomely adorned with carvings of this kind (*gachburi*). Among the pictures in Fath Ali's house were several of the Queen and of the Prince and Princess of Wales. I pointed these out, and answered questions about the royal family, the law of succession, and the number of wives permitted to a King of England. "Do you mean to say," asked the prophet, "that when your wife grows old and loses her beauty, you can't take another?" I assured him that such was the melancholy fact. The prophet then dilated upon his proper function, and explained, in verse, that with his permission the desert was safe for the traveller as a royal palace, but that if he gave the word for plunder, not ten thousand soldiers could protect the caravan; that when his congregation started on a raid, the heavens were too low for their feet to tread on, &c., &c. Fath Ali smiled, and told his beads. Talking about Islam in India, I mentioned Lucknow as a stronghold of the Persian or Shia faith, and spoke of the Najaf shrine there, named after the Najaf of pilgrimage, near Baghdad. Fath Ali broke silence. "*Khub nist,*" he said, "it is not good;" he would tolerate no mock shrines. We had sweetmeats and sherbet, and of course a qalyan, while dancing and singing were going on in the courtyard on which the room opened. The performers were boys, and the performance was perhaps one degree better than an Indian nautch; yet the audience listened with that rapt attention which is so inexplicable to a European. The prophet told me that in Seistan he had heard little Cabuli girls of nine or ten singing all night, on some festive occasion. All the company were lapped in motionless ecstasy till the dawning, when one of the little maids turned towards the east and sang,—

Ai subh ma ai, ki hanuz ast waqt i raz
Qissa i ashigan ta hanuz ast daraz;

"Dawn not, O morning, for it is the hour of secrecy still; the lovers' story is not half ended yet." Whereupon the whole company burst out weeping. It would be a powerful singer who could produce such an effect at a concert in London, for example.

The day after, in the evening, I called to bid Fath Ali good-bye. He was at his prayers, but the prophet welcomed me, and talked perhaps more freely than in his patron's presence. He told me of a friend of his, who had written to ask him for a rule of life, and he read me out his answer. It was in verse, and to this effect :— "You can go either to heaven or to hell, according as you choose your society. If you care for the company of straitlaced mullas and frouzy saints, you can find plenty of them in heaven. But hell is peopled with bold fellows, brave spirits, who have some fun in them. So make your choice. If you prefer heaven, go and sit with Muhammad and Ali *(birau, bâ Muhammad o Ali nashin)* beside the stream of Kausar, and drink its brackish water till you're tired *(bakhur har cha khwâhi az ân ab i shûr)*." Various other irreligious jokes were interspersed, over which the prophet laughed heartily, to my no small amazement. He recited verses cleverly and well; among others, a parody of his on an ode of Hafiz, where the love-lines of Hafiz alternated with interpolated lines of the prophet, perverting the praises of Hafiz' mistress into the praises of the prophet's thieves. Then the conversation turned on religion again, and I had to translate for him some of our prayers; I chose the Lord's Prayer, and the prayer for all sorts and conditions of men. Hereupon Fath Ali came in, and the prophet hastened to inform him that we Christians acknowledged the unity of God—that the prayers I had quoted were *tauhîd i khalis*, pure confession of God's oneness. But the upright Fath Ali was not so easily convinced. "Saint Jesus," said he, "never left you any prayer. *I* know; I have read your New Testament through, and there are no prayers prescribed in it, nor any system of religion (*sharîat*). Now, what do you believe concerning Saint Jesus? Do you believe Him to be God or man?" "We believe Him to be God," said I, "but there is a small sect who believe Him to be man only." "They believe right," said Fath Ali. "And what is your view of the crucifixion? Do you believe that Saint Jesus was crucified, or only a simulacrum (*surat*) of Him?" I felt I was getting rather out of my depth in theology, but proceeded to state what I considered the orthodox doctrine. "That's wrong," said Fath Ali. "It was only a simulacrum that was crucified, while Saint Jesus ascended to heaven there and then, not after His pretended resurrection, as you vainly talk. Nay, *we* have a higher reverence for Saint Jesus than you, who say that He was subjected to crucifixion." The conversation afterwards turned on India, and here again I found it impossible to convince Fath Ali that I was right in believing India to be part of the British possessions.

An old eunuch lighted me home. He was a travelled old fellow, and seemed anxious to apologize for his master's religious straitness. He had been to Bombay with Fath Ali's son, who went to consult an English doctor about a chronic complaint. They stayed there six months. The doctor used to call his patient a barbarian (*jangali admi*); I saw the young man myself, and do not wonder at it.

Sayyid Ali was unfortunately ill while he was in Lar; otherwise, being a kindred spirit, he might have fraternized with the prophet. He wrote the prophet a letter, to which the latter replied by an amusing medley of prose and rhyme, including a sacrilegious travesty of a verse of the Koran,[1] and ending by lamenting his own fate, to be in the hands of donkeys (*dar dast i kharán*), an allusion to Fath Ali, who had kept him two years.

In truth, Lar is not the place for a man of education. The principal topic of conversation

[1] The prophet explained to me with great glee how he had named his old wife "Mother of Robbers" (*ummu-sáriqin*) in imitation of the title, Mother of the Faithful, bestowed on the wife of Muhammad.

seems to be highway robbery. It is difficult to estimate how far this sort of talk is warranted by facts, and how far it is mere bravado. The number of soldiers seems to indicate an unstable state of security. Lar has a garrison of thirty artillerymen, with six guns. The guns were stowed in the verandah of the Bagh-i-Nishat, so I had opportunities of inspecting them. They are one 12-pounder, one 9-pounder, and four 6-pounders; all bronze guns. Four were cast in Tabriz, and two in Enzeli by a Tabriz workman. The 9-pounder is in a parlous state of dissidence at the mouth. The captain marshalled his men to do me honour. Far more numerous, however, are the irregular forces of Fath Ali Khan. The Lar men pride themselves on being *zaring*—a word which may be the same as the classical Persian *zîrak*, sharp or alert—and boast that Fath Ali needs no regulars, being always able to raise an adequate force on the spot. And certainly Lar is full of tufangchis—" every man with his flask of powder, and his firelock on his shoulder "— who stalk around as if each man were a host in himself. Their weapons are almost all percussion, and sometimes double-barrelled. Their discourse is of robbers and robbery.

On the other hand, the state of trade shows that the roads cannot be very unsafe. A caravan of 500 camels was expected in Lar the day after my departure. Lar has trade with Bombay through the three ports of Linga, Bandar Abbas, and Tahiri. I met a man who spoke some Hindustani; and a rude drawing of a ship on the walls of the Bagh-i-Nishat testified to the familiarity of the Lar youth with the idea of a sea-voyage. There are some well-to-do merchants in the city. One of them sent letters for me safely to India *viâ* Bandar Abbas.

The sights of Lar are as follows:—(1) The principal mosque, a stone building 30 feet high, enclosing a courtyard about 30 yards square, and having its walls decorated with plain blue tiles. (2) A small stone caravan-sarai, now in ruins. (3) The fort on one of the two hills behind the town. It is a steep limestone hill, 150 feet high, and once was girdled by fortifications; but there remains now only a small mud fort on the crest, garrisoned by a single family of tufangchis. A small broken cannon lay before the door. On the hill-side, below the fort, stands a small square building, stone-built, with a dome; this is said to be the tomb of Nadir Shah's mother.

So mighty a conqueror might have built his mother a statelier monument. Near this are two Persian baths excavated in the rock, also a third underground room, apparently for stores, and a well sunk 200 feet deep through the limestone. (4) The *qadamgah* or shrine on the opposite hill, with its abambar built to catch the drainage from the hill-top. (5) The old market, said to have been built by the same architect as designed the existing bazar at Herat. This has been commended as equal to the bazar of Shiraz, but really falls far short of it in design, and is entirely desolate at present. The shape is the usual one of four equal arms radiating from a circular and domed centre. Each arm is 60 yards long by 14 feet broad, and its vaulted roof is about 22 feet high, while the dome may be 10 feet higher. On each side was a row of shops, on a plinth raised some four feet above the roadway. Each shop had a depth of about six feet, and behind it was a closet which served as a storeroom. The arrangement of the shops in each of the four arms was, of course, precisely the same. The arms are built of unhewn stone, the dome of hewn stone, and round the inside, just under the springing of the dome, runs a long inscription, mostly illegible; but the verse containing the date can be made out as follows :—

Tarîkh-ash az khirad talabidand ; jawab guft
Dâr ul amán i Lar ihyá shud az in binai.[2]

The bazar is now wholly untenanted, and the roof of one arm has partly fallen. Near it stands a roofed cistern of water, in the shape of a cross. The Lar folk are very proud of these relics, and believe that similar cisterns stood at the end of all four arms in courtyards where camels could cast their loads; but I doubt if the design was ever completed. They say also that Lar had a race-course, and there are, in fact, certain pillars on the plain south of the town, which may have served to mark out a course.

Lar is said to have about 1200 inhabited houses. The population may be 6000. There is one slender qanat, with brackish water, and the well-water is also brackish. The wells have usually two, and sometimes three pulleys on one axle, and two or three pairs of bullocks working together; the water lies sixty to seventy feet below the surface. It

[2] The meaning of the couplet is, "They asked its date of wisdom; she made answer, 'Lar's house of safety was resuscitated by this building.'"

is perhaps needless to say that the town is full of abambars. Some of the merchants' houses are well-built and comfortable enough, but all present an exterior of mud, and the whole town, viewed from the limestone hills, looks low and grey. It has had a poor mud wall, which has now fallen away for the most part.

My quarters in the Bagh-i-Nishat were very comfortable. They faced a broad courtyard and garden, with a fine tank. Fath Ali sent provisions for me and all my people during the first day of my stay; but I determined to pay for my food on the second day. I bought three bottles of wine, which on being opened subsequently proved to be excellent vinegar.

The truffles of Lar are very good eating; they are found in the plain, under little heaps of earth, which give them their name of *dumbal i-zamin* or earth-boils. They are also called *aghír*, a local name.

Sayyid Ali having consulted a doctor, professed himself ready to start. His ailment was simply super-abundant fat, aggravated by compulsory walking exercise on the bad roads of the last few marches. We left Lar at dawn, with the pleasing certainty of a long and hot march before us.

CHAPTER VIII.

LAR TO SAIDABAD.

SIXTY-FIVE FARSAKHS: TEN DAYS.

26th March, Kahna, 8 farsakhs; 7 a.m. to 5 p.m.—I awoke at four in the morning, roused the servants, and returned to snatch an hour's sleep while the mules were packing. The servants immediately went to sleep again, as is the habit of Persian servants when the master's eye is withdrawn for a moment. We did not start till seven. The Lar plain runs nearly east and west, between low mountains, black and impregnated with salt; it is four miles wide, stony, and barren. In the neighbourhood of Lar are a few villages. At twelve miles we passed the ruins of Tanguni, with a small but well-built caravansarai, now untenanted; the qanat which gave life to the place has been choked some years. Here the plain proper ends in a tangle of dry watercourses and ravines, which extend ten miles, and then smooth themselves out into the plain of Aliabad, a circular area surrounded by black rocky hills, with Aliabad village in a tamarisk grove in the middle. Here the Forg and Hormuz roads diverge; we left Aliabad three miles on the right, and turned northward, after breakfasting beside an abambar, whence we could see the great dark mass of Hormuz mountain far to the east, and the nearer cliffs of Karmasta, streaked with salt. We entered the basin of a salt river, and presently caught sight of Kahna from afar, a black date-grove against a low range of limestone hills. The village fort contains about fifteen families. It belongs to Fath Ali, who bought it ten years ago, and has spent money in repairing the qanat. The wall of the fort is in good repair. We found the interior crowded with tufangchis, bringing revenue from Forg. They were loud on the subject of robbers, the insecurity of the road, and the extraordinarily daring and desperate character of the population hereabouts; altogether, an evil and unsavoury lot of rascals. My quarters were in a dilapidated straw shed. Sayyid Ali was partly in a state of collapse, believing that the atmosphere of the salt country aggravated his ailment.

27th March, Shahghaib, 7 farsakhs; 5.30. *a.m. to* 2.30 *p.m.*—We were off next morning an hour before dawn. I vainly tried to induce some of the tufangchis to accompany us for a reasonable reward. We had to march four miles to the left, to turn the limestone hills; then we entered a narrow valley full of ravines and knolls of limestone, and with three or four little streams of bitter water. This lasted ten miles, till we crossed the northern ridge of the valley, and after a couple of miles among low spurs and bluffs, coloured white and red, we came upon a small green table-land, and beheld an extraordinary prospect. Before and below us, from left to right, stretched a plain five miles wide, backed by black mountains seamed with glittering veins of salt, and breaking at their bases into little hillocks and runlets of pure salt, sparkling in the sun. A broad white stream of salt ran down the middle of the plain, and towards the right hand it expanded into a lake, the intense whiteness of which was heightened by contrast with the black rocks beyond. The utter desolation of the prospect had a strange charm of its own. Perhaps it was this very wildness and remoteness from humanity that persuaded the holy man, Shah Ghaib, to choose the margin of the salt lake as his home in life and death.

His shrine was to be our resting-place that night; and after a brief meal beside the abambar on the table-land (it is wonderful how cool and good the water keeps in these abambars) we descended and followed the border of the lake for eight hot and windless miles. The blue dome of the shrine shone against the dark background, and a scrap of Tennyson haunted me, keeping time to the paces of my horse, as rhymes will do when one is weary:—

> And underneath the blazing vault,
> Sown in a wrinkle of the monstrous hill,
> The city sparkles like a grain of salt.

The keeper of the shrine received us hospitably. We were a numerous party, for we had picked up tufangchis on the road. In the middle of the ravines, a poor pedestrian who had attached himself to my caravan for safety, came running back with uplifted hands, vowing that mounted Turks stopped the way. My muleteers, however, remained profoundly undisturbed; so, taking heart of grace, I rode on, and found seven men with guns, not mounted at all, and no Turks, but some of Fath Ali's tufangchis, who were going to Murz to bring back cattle of his to Lar. As they were going our way we easily induced them to join us.

The alarmist, of course, was unmercifully chaffed. He had, however, done some service in suggesting to me an answer to the puzzling question—where can the robbers come from? Possibly the small and sparsely-scattered villages of this unpeopled region may harbour a few bad characters; but it seems that the nomad Kashkais are the chief object of dread. They get the credit of making raids at great distances from their pasture-grounds; and the unsettled habits of the tribe render it easy, no doubt, to set up a good *alibi*.

Shah Ghaib's shrine is an oblong stone building, 16 feet high, by 24 long and 15 broad, with a conical blue-tiled dome at one end, which raises the height of the building to 35 feet. Shrine and dome are in good repair, thanks to Fath Ali. The space before the shrine is paved with the tombstones of persons whose bodies have been brought, after death, to lie near that of the saint. Some of these tombstones are of green marble, with rhyming inscriptions handsomely cut. Shah Ghaib was brother of Shah Chiragh of Shiraz, and thus related, in what degree I know not, to one of those extremely holy persons, the Imams.

The mutawalli or guardian of the shrine is not badly off. He has a number of goats and cows, and a small cornfield. An abambar gives him water. Last year it ran dry, and he and his family had to drink the brackish and sickening water of a well. Remains of a qanat, choked twenty years ago, can also be traced. The neighbourhood of the shrine is clothed with tamarisk and kunar. From the edge of this little space of level ground, a nearer view is obtained of the salt lake, the salt hills, hazy with heat, and one high mountain beyond, whose lower slopes discharge themselves into the lake in a torrent of peaks and ravines. Our host complained of raids by cattle-lifting Turks, but acknowledged that he had not been troubled in this way for the last two years. He had never left the shrine since the day he succeeded his father as mutawalli. In the summer months, when the abambars on the road are dry, weeks often pass without a visitor to this lonely spot. Yet, though thus cut off from the world by necessity and religious duty, the man was no fanatic. He talked with me freely and intelligently, gave me the best room in his house (it was a high open archway), and his wife brought me buttermilk and cooked my dinner. They killed a couple of kids for us, and I never tasted better meat in my life.

28th March, Fadumi, 9 farsakhs; 5 a.m. to

5 *p.m.*—An hour and a half before dawn we began the descent to the salt lake, crossed the stream that flows from its lower end, and marched to the foot of a black mountain range. Leaving this on the left, the road wound among low spurs, and came down on a little river, full of clear water coursing over stones covered with salt crystals. Crossing this we ascended into a small green plain, a welcome sight after the desolation of the last two marches. On our left, in a hollow of the black mountains, the fields and houses of Chahnar could be seen. A roofless abambar stood in the plain. We filled our bottles, crossed the plain, and entered the salt hills again. The road twisted curiously among ravines and stony knolls, between mountains higher than we had seen since leaving Lar. In one place, we marched along a narrow spur, with a gulf 100 feet deep on either hand. "Hell and Heaven" they call it (*duzakh o bihisht*), in allusion to that razor-edged bridge of Sirat, by which the faithful have to cross the infernal abysses and enter Paradise. Gradually ascending, we crossed a saddle-back, and saw a long plain sloping away from us, covered with grass and flowers, and green with tamarisk and kunar at its farther end. In the middle of the salt-hills we had found two pools

of rainwater,[1] in a hollow of the rocks, but we were all thirsty again by the time we reached the end of the plain and came upon a dry river-bed, which nevertheless contained a water-hole with brackish water. Four miles more over broken ground brought us in view of the wide plain of Murz, with its spacious date-groves. We put up in the village of Fadumi, tired with a march which had lasted nearly twelve hours.

There was a difficulty in getting bread. The people declared that they had been living on the green herb of the field for months past. Certainly they were very clamorous in complaint. I invited some forty of the male population under the thatch which served me for shelter. My great pith hat, as usual, was the first curiosity for inspection; they thought it weighed ten pounds, and it hardly weighed as many ounces. Then the questioning began. Why was I travelling? Would I not tell them the *real* reason why I undertook all this trouble and expense? One or two old men, who had been to the coast, had heard the name of England. Of Russia they seemed to know nothing. They complained bitterly of misgovernment. "Oppression," said one of the

[1] They call rainwater *ab i rahmat*, water of mercy; an epithet suggestive of a rainless country.

elders, "has gone on rising like a flight of steps (*pila mikhurad ta bala mirasad*). We were never so misgoverned in the old days; what have we done to be so afflicted now? Perhaps no country in the world is so badly governed as this. Why, when we look at your caravan and your goods (*dastgah*), we marvel how you have come here safely through the thieves." And then I was asked to represent the facts to the Shah, when I reached Teheran. Complaints to the Mutamid, they said, only made matters worse. At last the most respectable inhabitant said, "I wish your people would come up from the sea like a flood, and take the country. We should all be content." I promptly disavowed any intention of annexation, and presently the assembly broke up, one lad remarking, as he turned away, "So *that's* a Farangi; and that's his hat."

29th March, Forg, 3 farsakhs; 7 a.m. to noon.—The Murz plain is watered from a stream of sweet water which descends from the plain of Forg, and falls into the salt river we had crossed, rendering its water tolerable for irrigation. There are only three villages in the plain. We had the choice of two roads to Forg; one up the defile through which the Forg water flows, and one round the eastern end of the mountain-range which that defile intersects. We chose the latter, as the defile had an evil reputation. Our tufangchis, being unable to go beyond Murz, were paid off and dismissed. We called at Murz village on our way, and asked the kalantar for a guard. He gave us half a dozen tufangchis, and sent his son also with us, mounted on a good grey horse. I walked nearly the whole way; it was only twelve miles, and my horses had already begun to suffer from sore backs. The eastern end of the mountains is a great scarped peak, 1000 feet above the road, called King Nureddin's fort, but nobody knows who Nureddin was, nor could I see any traces of fortification on the summit. We crossed a low ridge among stony hills, with a spring of bitter water at the top, quite drinkable, but tasting as if it were full of drugs. In the descent we saw a man coming our way. So rare a sight threw the whole escort into commotion. We crowned the heights with horse and foot, and discovered nobody, except this solitary pedestrian carrying flour to Murz. Forg plain now lay before us, well-watered and green, with high dark mountains on its farther side, and the date-groves of villages dotted over its surface.

The town of Forg, so to call it, is surrounded by a mud wall in the form of a square, with a side of perhaps 400 yards, armed with round towers at regular intervals. It had four tall gates, and a governor's residence inside; but these are all ruined and deserted now. Date-trees and mud-houses, more or less dilapidated, fill the space between the walls. We went to the governor's house. He proved to be a nephew of Fath Ali, and gave me good quarters in a carpeted upper room, while my caravan found room below. Near his house is an old Husainia[2] of unhewn stone, with a few mulberry-trees and the remains of a tank. Forg has been a place of some importance in past years. A mile south of the town stands an old fort called after Bahman, with three rows of walls and ditches girdling a rocky hill, the summit of which is crowned with towers and vaulted rooms. The fort is built of stone, but is a ruin now. Another fort occupies a flat space on the slope of the hills six miles south-west of Forg; it is

[2] A Husainia is an enclosure, better or worse provided with buildings, in which the people of the town or village assemble on certain religious occasions, notably for the miracle-play on the anniversary of the deaths of Hasan and Husain. It corresponds to the *imambara* of Indian Mussalmans.

called Shah Marz's fort, and has almost disappeared; but a stone platform where Shah Marz used to sit is still in good preservation. Forg itself seems never to have had guns, but its mud fortifications are not contemptible. The plain is sanctified by two shrines, one four miles south-east, the other two miles east of the town; they belong respectively to Shah Muhammad, brother of Shah Chiragh, and to Zachariah, brother of the Imam Riza himself. Both have small blue domes, and are endowed with dategroves and water. The plain gets a good supply of water from a qanat from the eastern mountains, and from the perennial stream of the Tang i Abdu, towards the north. The governor has jurisdiction as far as Ahmadi and Fin to the south-east, and Gishkuh in the direction of Saidabad. He was extremely friendly, gave me a good dinner, and brought the notables of the place to converse with me. They asked me endless questions about England, which I answered to the best of my ability in the space of two hours.

30th March, Chagunu tents, 5 farsakhs; 7 a.m. to 5 p.m.—I could get no clear information concerning the direct road to Saidabad, except that it was a very bad one. The unanimous advice of the assembly was that I should go either *via* Tarum on the south-east, or Rostak on the north-west; but I had had enough of salt and heat,[3] and determined to ascend the Tang-i-Abdu and march across the mountains. "You will repent it," said a grave old worthy; "the laden mules can never get up." But having paid the muleteers up to date, and given them a small advance to carry on with, I found them quite prepared to face the difficulties of the pass. The governor wanted me to stay one day more in Forg; but finding that I had to go, he gave me tufangchis, and we marched for the redoubtable pass. We tracked the stream upwards to the mouth of the gorge, passing two mills[4] on our way, and rejoicing to see green banks and fresh water after so many brackish waterholes and glittering streams of salt. Inside the gorge we found a tumbled mass of rocks, among which the stream made its way, between cliff-walls 300 to 400 feet high.

[3] The heat by day was nevertheless far less vexatious than in India at the same time of the year; and the nights were always cool.

[4] Persian mills are on the turbine plan so familiar in the Indian hills, until one gets as far north as Isfahan, where the upright breast wheel comes in. The diameter of the wheel never exceeds four feet.

The musical joyous water, the fresh mountain breeze, the sunlight and shade on rocky pinnacles and steeps, the jangle of the mule-bells, and the very effort of climbing towards cooler regions, all tended to raise one's spirits and awaken a lively sense of present pleasure. Along the side of the cliffs could be traced the remains of a road, which we had to follow in one place for a few yards. Here one of the mules came down, and almost went over the edge with his load. The fall would have been forty feet. One of my horses, which was following the caravan, had a similar escape. The pass narrowed as it rose, and ended in a slanting path up a steep incline of rocky detritus, crowned by 200 feet of sheer cliff. At the foot of the cliff is a small spring, called Ali's Well. Here we halted, unloaded, and carried the loads up a natural flight of stairs (and very irregular stairs too), 150 feet high, in the face of the cliff, to a ledge where it was possible to load up again. While the mules were loading, I enjoyed the fresh air and the view. The stream seemed to sleep in lucent blue pools 300 feet below us, shut in, like ourselves, by great walls and towers of rock. On our right the cliff rose highest, and at its foot an isolated spire of rock, which the country people call Ali's pulpit. They believe that Ali used to say his prayers here after bathing in one of the pools below, which goes by the name of his *hammam*. But the beauty of the place can stand on its own merits, and defy the son-in-law of the Prophet.

After this the road rises over the mountain-tops, among camel-thorn and almond bushes, with here and there a stunted mastich-tree. The rounded heights and shelving valleys afford a wide prospect of little variety, but breathed over by fresh invigorating air. We were in search of an encampment of nomads, and, as usual, we failed to find it till near sunset. The place is called Châgunu, and the nomads are not Turks, but Persians; indeed, they are dwellers in tents rather than nomads, for they have no separate and distant summer and winter quarters, but remain on these half-way mountain-tops all the year round, in what might be called a temperate climate. They have orchards and vineyards on the southern slopes; we passed some on our way. The difference between these people and the Turks is noteworthy. They are much more inquisitive than Turks, more talkative, forward, fond of joking, and somewhat given to braggadocio.

But they were most hospitable to me and my party, pitched a good white tent for me, and a black tent for Sayyid Ali, and gave us all a capital dinner of kid's flesh. After dinner the men crowded into the tent to "interview" me. There was not much to be learned from their conversation, and they evidently disbelieved most of what I had to tell them. It was plain, however, that they were contented, and had no complaints to make. Sayyid Ali told me next day that he had been much gratified by their expressions of loyalty to the Shah—a subject on which, of course, I had not attempted to sound them. The yoke of government (or misgovernment) sits much easier on the nomad than on the villager, who is tied down to his fields, and may find himself at the mercy of a petty tyrant.

31st March, Dehistan, 5 farsakhs ; 7 a.m. to 2 p.m.—Next day we descended the back of the mountains, down a long gently-sloping plateau, to a small half-brackish river which waters three small villages, with the help also of a qanat led from the northern heights. Riding on in advance, I called at one of these villages, in the belief that it was our destined halting-place. I was wrong; but the villagers insisted on my staying to smoke a qalyan.

They brought me breakfast also—soup, bread, dates, and buttermilk, in return for which I had to tell them all I could about Farangistan, and to listen to their grievances. It was the old story of undue revenue exactions, and I was struck by their using the same figure of gradually ascending stairs which had been used by the men of Fadumi. Hospitality is common in Persia, but here was a case where its genuineness could hardly be questioned, for I was alone and at some distance from the road. I overtook the caravan at the gates of our halting-place, and found Sayyid Ali in a state of disgust. The kalantar did not want us, pleaded insufficiency of provisions, and paid no respectful attention to our letters from Lar and Forg. We were advised to go to Dehistan, two miles further on, a place represented as well-stocked and charming. Marching through a little gorge, the sides of which were lined in parts with apple and pear trees in luxuriant bloom, we came upon a tiny plain covered with date-palms, in the middle of which stood the village fort. Here we met a Persian gentleman bound, like us, for Saidabad, but by a different route. We asked and answered some questions, and then entered Dehistan. The kalantar proved disobliging, though not openly uncivil; he would do nothing to help us to provisions or quarters, and we had to put up in the house of the Mulla of the village—a man of Karman, who had some education and much liberality. Poor Sayyid Ali enjoyed little peace in this place, where nothing was to be bought but after desperate haggling. I watched him bargaining for eggs with a preternaturally sharp urchin of seven years, who exacted twopence halfpenny per egg, gave us bad money in change, and disappeared. We had to lay in provisions for three marches, and to engage a guide to take us across the mountains. And thereby hangs a tale.

Sayyid Ali had succeeded in making terms with a promising sort of man, who carried a gun and represented himself as a warrior of no mean repute, and who at any rate appeared to know the country thoroughly. But he was to be no guide of ours, so the Fates willed it; for in half an hour a messenger called him away to do battle for his lord. I had heard a few shots while I was writing, but thought nothing of them. The fact, however, was that two men had quarrelled over the ownership of a datepalm, and one had shot the other in the throat, killing him on the spot. The man thus killed belonged to the same village as my guide, and his kalantar espoused the quarrel, and took the field with his tufangchis to demand surrender of the murderer, who had fled to his own village of Behnu. So my guide was summoned away to join this expedition, and Sayyid Ali had to enlist a ragged fellow of doubtful capabilities. As it turned out, however, we were to want neither guide nor provisions.

1st April, Kaha, 5 farsakhs; 8 a.m. to 2.30 p.m.—Next morning we marched to Behnu. The road descends the Dehistan gorge (which contains a small stream, whence the Dehistan fields get their water) but soon crosses the ridge on the left, and enters a long plain, where stands the village of Behnu, watered by channels from the river we had seen the day before. A mile outside the village we met a party of sixteen armed men. They were the avengers of blood, who had been unable to break sanctuary; in other words, the kalantar of Behnu had shut his gates upon them, and now they talked of appealing to Fath Ali. The father and brother of the deceased were with them. The old man was weeping; the son's face showed chiefly a sullen consciousness of

A Siege.

injury unavenged. "Such a fine youth!" said one of the party, referring to the deceased. "He was worth 500 tomans." This reminded me of the sailors' song that begins *Five pound ten for an able man ;* but 500 tomans are about 200*l.*; and indeed in Kavar I had heard of two slain youths who were estimated at 1000 tomans each.

We marched on to Behnu, where the kalantar, seeing the laden mules and our peaceful array, opened his gates and came out with his musketeers, and we got buttermilk and bread, as well as the pleasure of a chat with the garrison. While we were eating, a servant trotted in on a mule. He belonged to the kalantar's brother, who is a major in the Persian army, and is also Ilbegi or chief of a tribe of Afshâr Turks, and who had been sent for yesterday, and was now coming, to see fair play in his brother's quarrel. We met the major himself as we left Behnu. He promised to overtake us that evening in Kaha, and to show us the way to his tents. We went on up a gorge which opens on the northern side of the Behnu plain. An old watchtower marks the place where tolls used to be collected thirty years ago. After some miles we came on pools of brackish water in the gorge, then a few scattered fields, a small village fort, and finally, built against the side of a hill, our halting-place of Kaha. I shall always remember Kaha as the most humble village I saw in Persia. The houses were like Irish hovels, built of the large grey stones which covered the hill-side. The best of these hovels was given to me. It was poor enough, but infinitely better than the kennel or burrow allotted to Sayyid Ali.

In the evening, I went out with some of the gilded youth of Kaha, to see an old fort on the top of a hill some 500 feet high. There were the remains of a rude stone wall, and of two water-cisterns, one of which had recently been repaired. The fort, they said, belonged to a Kafir monarch, and was taken by the Commander of the Faithful (*Amir ul Muminîn*), but they evidently had no clear notion as to who the latter sacred personage might be. In the cliff below the fort there is a small cave, which is credited with endlessness, like all other caves in this country,[5] and is further remarkable for

[5] M. Khanikoff gives a marvellous account of the cave above Taft, from the story told him by a Persian who tried to explore it. The cave at Shahpur is said to have an exit at Persepolis, sixty miles away. As a matter of fact Dr. Odling went to the end of it last spring, and estimated its length at 400 yards.

harbouring a dragon (*azhdahá*) who guards the buried treasure of the deceased Kafir, and comes down every Friday night to drink of the stream in the valley (usually dry), and to kill and devour any man he may happen to meet; this done, he returns to his cave. The Kaha boys were anxious that I should exercise the well-known power of Farangis, and discover the hidden hoard; also, that I should cure a little girl of epilepsy. But I had to confess with shame that I was ignorant alike of medicine and divination. It was pitiful to witness their disbelief in my disclaimer with regard to the girl. They brought her to me, and went on pleading that to cure her would be an act of humanity (*muruwwat*) and a good work (*sawáb*), as if religious scruples held my healing hand. They questioned me about my religion. How did I say my prayers? —a question which one cannot easily answer without losing some degrees in public estimation, for Mussalmans, being wedded to a ceremonial religion, are inclined to doubt the reality of a religion which does not prescribe fixed hours and postures and formulæ for private prayer.

The Kaha people, however, were evidently no theologians. Their belief was in Hazrat Abbas and the Commander of the Faithful (whoever he might be); the name of Muhammad they did not seem to have heard. I was questioned as to my belief in these two worthies, and explained that Farangistan knew nothing of them, and therefore did not repudiate them, but stuck to what it believed to be the Gospel for the West, leaving the Gospel for the East (*mashraq zamin*) to stand on its own merits. From religion we came to matrimony. Was I married? Was it true that Farangi wives had their will by night, on condition of submitting to the husband's will by day? Not being a married man, I was unable to answer the latter question. Then came politics. Was there peace between my Shah and the Shah of Persia? I assured them that the mutual relations were most friendly. If they were to fight, which side did I consider likely to win? I thought to evade this point diplomatically, by observing that fortunately there was no danger of a breach of friendship; but the Kaha militia had already formed their opinion on the subject. "You won't be angry, now," they asked, "if we tell you what *we* think? If we fought with your people, we should win, because we are smarter (*zirangtar*) than you, and one of us could kill seven or eight of your men." "But remember," said I, "that we have cannons." "The cannons don't matter," was the reply, "we are so smart." Fired by these warlike thoughts, one of the band endeavoured to discharge his gun, but after wasting three caps, and vainly trying to clear the nipple with a straw, he gave up the attempt.

The elders conversed more gravely, and complained much of misgovernment. "Did you ever see such a ruined place (*kharába*)?" they asked, pointing to their poor village. What seemed to weigh most upon them (and I had noticed the same thing elsewhere) was the (alleged) impossibility of obtaining redress of grievances. "To whom should we appeal? The Padshah knows nothing of this remote village. Fath Ali has ruined the country; he takes everything, and does nothing. If my brother were killed, and I demanded blood-money or the surrender of the murderer, Fath Ali would accept 100 tomans from my adversary, and I should be dismissed as a liar." And then came again the question which had surprised me in Fadumi, "Why don't your people come and govern the country?"

The Ilbegi arrived before sunset. I went to

see him, and drank tea there. He was anxious that we should be his guests next day. "There is a little danger," he said, "on the march, but, *inshallah*, we shall arrive safely." The danger, I fancy (such as it was), threatened him and his people only; it was possible that the relatives of the murdered man might seek to satisfy the law of retaliation by lying in wait for the life of the brother of the murderer's master. Somebody in Kaha said of the Ilbegi, *dushman dárad*, "he has an enemy;" but if the fact was so, it did not seem to trouble him much. We arranged that my caravan should set out before dawn if possible, and wait for the Ilbegi's party at a place dalled Bâgha, about ten miles on the way. I warned the Ilbegi that my mules could not keep pace with his light horsemen, but he seemed to value my company more than expedition. It was with satisfaction that I learned from him that the whole of the next day's march was to be up a gentle slope, lifting us out of the region of the date-palm. It was evident, indeed, that we were now entering on a country of high mountains. From Chagunu we had seen the snowy outlines of the Kuh-i-Khabr on the northeastern horizon, and snow could be seen also in patches on the dark mountains which seemed to start up in the far distance on the right hand and the left, as we advanced farther into the land. The hill I climbed at Kaha gave me a good view of the Kuh-i-Siyah to the south, black, jagged, and in shadow, and the Bukhun mountains to the south-east, snow-crowned, and lighted by the evening sun. To the north extended long slowly-rising moors; but it must be remembered that on a Persian moor camel-thorn[6] takes the place of heather, furze, or broom, and stones take the place of grass.

Kaha is watered from a stream which descends a long strath in these moors, joins the Behnu river, and ultimately finds its way to the sea. When I saw it, the bed was broad and stony, and the water scanty. After an hour's rain the upper courses began to fill, and the silver gleam of the descending flood could be seen from the old fort. The men with me called to those below, in the sustained chanting tone which sends the voice so far in mountain regions of still clear air. *Rudkhána ámad,* they cried, " the river is coming;" but the

[6] It is like a tiny furze bush, but grey rather than green. In spring it breaks out into the loveliest white bells, like those of the convolvulus. It makes capital fire-wood, and has a very pleasant aromatic smell.

rain had been insufficient, and the river never arrived.

2nd April, Tents at Naukan, 10 *farsakhs ;* 6.30 *a.m.* to 7 *p.m.*—Before sunrise we were marching over the moors. We had the end of a range of hills on our left, and an isolated hill on our right, behind which lay the village of Gishkuh,⁷ the last village of the Shiraz province in this direction. Gishkuh, they said, was deserted; its people had fled to Aliabad. We now saw a broad moor before us, backed by a high distant ridge. On its hither side a tower and an orchard told us of Bagha—and breakfast. In the tower were three women, who denied the possession of any earthly goods, even of buttermilk. A tiny spring, whose waters are collected into a pool, keeps alive an acre of wheat, and the orchard of apple, pear, apricot, and plum-trees which gives the place its name. While breakfasting here we were joined by the Ilbegi, who gave me some *halwa*

---

[7] " Mountain of wild oleander." The shrub is said to be poisonous. Muleteers bound from Saidabad to Bandar Abbas take a branch of wild oleander when they come to Gishkuh, and beat their mules with it, saying, *gish, gish*. The result is that the mules abstain from cropping the poisonous shrub, though they will eat almost anything.

that agreeably eked out my meal of bread and dates. Thence we marched together over the long undulations of the slope, towards the ridge slowly drawing nearer. I looked back as we began the ascent, and could retrace the day's march over what now seemed a broad and level plain. I was looking southwards; on my left the wide moors stretched away to the bases of the Kuh-i-Khahr, whose huge irregular form, robed in snow, had been seen by glimpses since the morning, but now stood forth complete; while straight before me the sawlike ranges of the southern mountains girt the horizon with a black wall rising in successive tiers. It was my last look over the lower mountain-lands of Fars. We crossed the ridge, wound our way through the broken country on its farther slope, and suddenly, on the rounding of a hill, discovered a novel, and to me very wonderful prospect. A vast plain *(kafa)* lay before us, perfectly flat, utterly bare; it began at the foot of the hills, and lost itself afar in the warm haze of the mirage. Into this sea, as it were, the last mountains, sullenly retiring westwards, threw out spurs and promontories, enclosing harbours and long creeks. We seemed to be riding down the beach of some great tidal estuary, to which the waters should soon return. I almost looked to see the wave-lines and seaweed at our feet. On the horizon stood a lonely rock, an Ailsa Craig in this dry firth. That marked Abbasabad, our next day's stage; but meanwhile where were the Ilbegi's tents? We marched along the shore for two hours before we overtook his people, who were shifting their encampment. The sun had sunk behind the black hills before we reached the new camping-ground. The Ilbegi gave us good tents and a good dinner, in return for which I showed him my guns. He was very anxious to buy one of them, offering money, horses, mules, or camels in exchange. His tribe was said to consist of 5000 families, probably far too high an estimate. They were on their march, by slow stages, to their summer pasture-grounds in the mountains of Chahar-Gumbaz and Lalazar.

Our march to-day lasted more than twelve hours, and must have covered nearly forty miles.

3rd April, Abbasabad, 5 farsakhs; 8.30 a.m. to 2.30 p.m.—I bade good-bye to the Ilbegi with hearty thanks, and set out soon after sunrise for Abbasabad. We marched across the plain. At fourteen miles we came on a stream of fresh water, and breakfasted. I was disappointed at not having to cross the *kavîr*, but at any rate we could see it, like a white strip under the western hills. Perhaps it may be well to explain what a Persian *kavîr* is. It is the result of the bareness of Persian mountains, and the saline virtues of a Persian plain. The mountains, being destitute of trees, brushwood, or grass, have for centuries been wearing away under sun, wind, and rain; the crumbled rocks extend in long smooth slopes down to the plain, while a long smooth slope rises again to the hills on the opposite side. Such a slope will often be twenty miles broad. The rain and snow of winter, descending from the hills in streams small and great, lose themselves in these porous slopes, and emerge again at the lowest level of the plain, but in a far different shape. The water has become full of salt, and oozes up to the surface in patches of glittering white. Thus a kavîr must always follow the drainage line of the plain in which it happens to lie, and if the plain be a large one, the kavîr may be seen like a white strip stretching away in the direction in which the plain falls, till plain and kavîr are lost in the sky. For the rest, the quantity of water in a kavîr varies at different times and in different places, so that you may have either a mere saline efflorescence on good firm clay, or a salt quagmire in which the laden beast will founder if it strays off the track. Small pools of brackish waters are not uncommon, sometimes with a few tamarisk bushes; but the general aspect of a kavîr is utter bareness, unbroken by stone or weed. The smallest object, they say, shows in vastly magnified proportions; if there happens to be a clod on the surface, it looks like a hill. I have seen something like this, but not invariably, nor to the extent related.

We were now in the Sirjan district, the capital of which is Saidabad. It is a large and flourishing district, at the head of the great plain or valley which extends north-westwards towards Isfahan. It is watered by qanats drawn from the eastern mountains, and fed by the snows of the distant and lofty ranges of Chahar-Gumbaz, Hazar, and Lalazar, whose white sides and summits were noble features in the landscape to the east and south, as we marched to Abbasabad and Saidabad. Beyond Saidabad, the range of irrigation is exhausted, and the plain becomes a desert. Abbasabad is the most southern village of the district. We

Abbasabad.

found it a very small place, with dome-roofed houses, a style of building affected in the Sirjan district and in many other parts of Persia, perhaps by reason of the scarcity of wood. The people were Turks reclaimed from nomadism; consequently, the women did not veil their faces, and I had my first opportunity of conversing with the fair sex of the country. The remains of my Muscat *halwa* served to put matters on a good footing between me and the children, and I was presently surrounded by the whole female population of the place, eager to see my table, chair, bed, clothes, and anything else that I could show them. Two of the young women were good-looking, and one of the two (*ætat* 22) was recommended to me as being very clever (*zaring*); so I gave her a coat of mine to mend, which had been torn that morning by a horse putting his foot on it as it fell off the saddle. I lent her a needle and thread, and she made a very workmanlike job of the rent. She begged the gift of the needle in return, and got it. Then I went out to bathe. A woman showed me the way to the qanat, and came back when I was dressing, to express a hope that I had enjoyed my bathe. I was quartered under a domed archway which formed part of the house of an old woman. My hostess was most assiduous in her attentions. Towards evening she came to me with many apologies, and explained that one of the carpets was needed for the children to sleep on, if I could spare it. Of course the carpet was promptly surrendered. Yet this estimable old lady sold us a fowl which, on being opened, proved to be blue and green inside, having, in fact, been long known to be languishing under mortal disease; and we could neither get another nor recover our money. The men did not come home from the fields till late in the day. After dark I joined a party of men and women round a fire, and was asked the same question as at Kaha about the relations between husband and wife in Europe.

4th April, Saidabad, 8 farsakhs; 7 a.m. to 4 p.m.—Next day we marched down the plain to Saidabad, went to the caravansarai, and sent Zaki Beg to the governor. He came back with the news that quarters would be ready for us in half an hour. They proved to be extensive mud premises, considerably in disrepair. In the evening I visited the governor, an amiable youth with a cast in one eye. His father had bought the farm of the revenue of Sirjan for

A Persian Banquet.

2000 tomans, the revenue being 26,000 tomans a year, exclusive of octroi. Arrears to the amount of 2000 tomans were now due, and the farmer (or governor) had gone to Karman to try to set matters square, leaving this son of his as governor *ad interim*. The young man was much more bent on amusing himself than on governing. He was a friendly and social specimen of the Shahzada, and particularly well educated in music; in all things else, entirely ignorant. He was even unacquainted with the geography of his district.

5th April, Halt at Saidabad.—He returned my visit next morning, and invited me to a small and select entertainment after dinner. I went. The manner of the entertainment was as follows:—A tray, placed on the floor, contained a bowl of sour milk and spinach, some bread, a few sweetmeats, and a bottle of arrack with a dirty rag as stopper. The bottle had once contained better stuff, to wit, Tivoli beer; and the tray also, by its tawdry colours and outrageous pattern, proclaimed its connexion with far Farangistan. Behind this regal array sat a musician with a five-stringed instrument, like a huge guitar. They call it *tár* in these parts; it is played with the finger, armed with a *mizrab* or small triangle of wire. The steel strings were not unmelodious, but the voice of the singer recalled those noises which make night hideous on the occasion of Indian weddings. My hopes of an ode of Hafiz, chanted *con espressione*, vanished as soon as the singer opened his mouth to bellow forth *Amân, Amân*, and *Yár, Yár*, till the roof shrieked again. I felt half inclined to say *Persicos odi, puer, apparatus*, and take my leave; but the rapt countenances of the Shahzada and his brother betrayed such an intense enjoyment as it would have been cruel to interrupt. Presently the princely hand withdrew the greasy stopper from the bottle, and offered me half a wine-glass of arrack. This is a colourless liquor made from the grape, as strong as brandy, and powerfully seasoned with aniseed. Having helped his guest, the Shahzada poured for himself, and afterwards for all the company, sending the single wine-glass round with great gravity. After drinking we ate bread with curds and spinach, till once more "music arose with its voluptuous swell." Sayyid Ali turned up at this stage of the proceedings, and respectfully

---

[8] "Mercy, mercy," and "Friend, friend." The word *friend*, of course, has a mystical reference to the Almighty, and an apparent reference to the singer's mistress.

Saidabad. 181

asked the Shahzada to favour us with some display of his musical talent. The Shahzada, delighted, turned up his cuffs, and laid hold of a red and black drum, shaped like a stage goblet, but half the size of a churn. Placing the stem of this under his left arm, this representative (somewhat remote) of Achæmenes and Chosroes proceeded to finger the parchment with no despicable dexterity to a tune called the Russian, faintly suggesting that high and moving composition which goes by the name of *Lanigan's Ball*. I applauded, and shortly after took my departure. When one has to march at sunrise there is some inconvenience in waiting to see the end of an Oriental *soirée musicale*. Sayyid Ali remained, and kept it up with the Shahzada till the small hours.

Saidabad town has some 8000 inhabitants. It is in good repair, possesses a decent covered bazaar, and has a comfortable and thriving appearance which is highly satisfactory to one coming out of poor famished Fars. The town has improved of late years. The people are well dressed, and are much fairer than those of the south; the children especially are rosy and pretty. Here one sees the genuine Persian dress—a tunic with skirts reaching nearly down to the knee, wide blue trousers, and a felt hat, which may be round and low, or cylindrical and as high as the English "chimney-pot" hat. The tunic opens as low as a dress waistcoat, and shows the white shirt underneath. It is a neat and seemly dress. The quiet orderly habits of the people are proved by the fact that in all Saidabad I saw but one tufangchi. In Lar I could not step out of doors without meeting half a dozen. As for the Sirjan district, of which Saidabad is the capital, it may be fifty miles long by twelve broad, and contains perhaps twenty villages, dotted over the centre of the plain, between the *Kavîr* and the long slopes through which the water filters from the eastern mountains. While we were there, snowy peaks could be seen on all four points of the compass. To the north were the mountains of Pariz (8000 feet) to the west those of Niriz (7400 feet), to the south Lalazar (15,000), to the east Chahar-Gumbaz (14,000).

There are two roads from Saidabad to Karman, one by Saadatabad, the other by Pariz. The former is well known; and as the site of Pariz is marked in the map with a note of interrogation, I determined to visit the place, though we should lose two days by taking that route.

CHAPTER IX.

SAIDABAD TO KARMAN.

FORTY-FOUR FARSAKHS: SEVEN DAYS.

6th April, Kurran, 7 farsakhs; 8 a.m. to 4 p.m.
—My second day in Saidabad had been rainy, and for nearly a fortnight longer the weather continued unsettled. We had not gone far on our way towards Kurran, when we were overtaken by a storm of rain and wind, which came sweeping over the bare plain with such fury that it fairly blew the mules to leeward, and made them halt for half an hour. My mackintosh kept me dry, but my hands and feet were numbed with the cold. Poor Sayyid Ali, enveloped in a thick but porous great-coat, looked like a wet hen; and the rest of my people, and the baggage, got thoroughly drenched. The rain cleared off about eleven, leaving a bracing cold air. In Kurran we found good quarters in the kalantar's house,

and fires to dry our things. The village is one of eight which belong to the descendants of a holy man, on whom they were bestowed in fee by the then ruling power. The descendants now number ninety-six souls. In the middle of the village is an open space with mulberry trees, where the water of the qanat comes out from underground and runs sparkling down the street. Some of the lanes are bordered by mulberry and willow, with a watercourse between. The village seems to have enjoyed a long term of tolerable fortune, yet the people said that the district was ruined (*Saidabad sukht*). Kurran has a large orchard of apples, pears, apricots, plums, pomegranates, and grapes. It has also much poppy cultivation, in fields enclosed by low walls, and very carefully irrigated. The crop has been introduced only within the last five years. It pays better than wheat, and now covers most of the old wheat lands. Another new crop was potatoes, but last year's drought left nothing to sow. I walked round the village with the people, led by an old gentleman whom they called by the title of Agha. They asked me whether I was an Englishman or a Russian; also about Shaikh Obaidullah and the Kurdish war, and whether the Sultan of Rum was not encouraging the Shaikh in his war with Persia. They were remarkably fair, well-built, and well-clothed, and betrayed a natural and liberal curiosity to see and speak with the Farangi.

7th April, Pariz, 3 farsakhs; 9 a.m. to 1 p.m. —I had a good bathe next morning in the tank of the courtyard, under two noble plane-trees (*chinar*), which were just beginning to put forth leaves. The march to Pariz was a short one, among the undulations at the base of the Pariz mountains, which yesterday's weather had clothed with an ampler coating of snow. To the north, far away, the mountains of Maimanda showed snowy white—a noble object, though their elevation cannot be great, and their whiteness was probably due to a casual snowstorm. We crossed some tiny rivulets among the hills, which water little hamlets hidden in fruit-trees. Pariz itself lies in a dell enclosed by four low hills. We came on it all of a sudden, and looked down with surprise on its compact array of flat grey roofs. A stream runs down the main street. Trees rise among the buildings, and in the upper hollows of the hills are orchards and vineyards. It is a quaintly situated and pleasant place, but the water dwindles away sadly in summer. On two of the highest hills above the village are two round towers for tufangchis; and on another is the ruin of a mud fort, square, with a ditch. We had a little trouble in finding quarters. Zaki Beg invaded the house of a widow, which was neat enough, but small. The people of the village recommended the Husainia, where room was not wanting, if one could dispense with roofs and doors. Sayyid Ali, however, hearing of an Akhund or schoolmaster, went to that learned man, and speedily persuaded him to take us in, while the mules were disposed of in the Husainia. The Akhund turned his women out, and gave me a very comfortable carpeted room. His old father had been to Baghdad and Mashhad several times. What seemed to strike him most in Baghdad was the tramway to Karbala. The rails he called *na'l*, the same term as is used for a horse-shoe. He asked me about European railways and steamboats; he himself had travelled by steamboat to Baghdad. I was glad to find that these outward and visible signs of European civilization were not unheard of in Pariz. Later on, Zaki Beg came to me with much formality, and begged to represent that a young person stood outside, desiring to consult me on medical matters. Being introduced, she proved to be a fine young woman, fair, and well dressed. She kept playing with her veil, but took care to let me see her face abundantly; it was decidedly good-looking. She wanted medicine, she said; any kind of medicine. But for what sort of ailment? To this I got no answer, except downcast looks and writing on the floor with her toes. Sayyid Ali entered upon an explanation. "This young person," said he, "is now in her six-and-twentieth year. She has had four husbands, who have successively died. She now desires a medicine which will enable her to procure a fifth husband." This soft impeachment the damsel did not attempt to deny. I regretted that I had neglected to provide myself with any medicine of that nature; and she retired in disappointment.

The Akhund's wife and daughters cooked me an excellent dinner, which was all the more acceptable as I had not been able to get any meat in Kurran, where the people had killed and thrown away all their fowls, on account of a real or imaginary worm in their stomachs, which made them unclean. But in Pariz, besides a fowl, I had two puddings, one of boiled rice, and one of ground rice, almonds, and sugar—thanks to these good women. They came to the door to see me eat, and stood there whispering in amazement during the half-hour given to dinner. My habit of reading at dinner never failed to excite the curiosity of any Persian who witnessed it. Why did I read, and what was I reading? These Mussalmans are so wrapped up in formulæ and ceremonies, that they are apt to attribute a religious significance to every act of a European which seems to them at all out of the common.

8th April, God-i-Ahmar, 5 farsakhs; 9 a.m. to 4 p.m.—We marched next day for God-i-Ahmar, or the Red Deeps. We had to cross the Pariz mountains, but not at their highest point; in fact, we turned the northern end of the range, and left the snow-covered peaks a mile or two on our right. On our left hand was a confused region of low hills. Behind us lay the broad plain of Sirjan; and before us, just seen for a moment beyond the hilly country yet to be crossed, was the plain of Rafsinjan. The belt of mountains and hills between these two plains is about fifty miles broad where we crossed it. Eastwards it becomes much broader, till it merges in the region of high table-lands and peaks of perennial snow which send waters down to fertilize the head of both the plains. Westwards it diminishes in breadth and in height, and the plains also lose their waters, and become empty and bare. We crossed three or four tiny streams, each with its little patch of cultivation and small orchard guarded by a peasant's hut. Near the end of the march we crossed a strong swift burnie flowing down towards Sirjan, full of white snow-water, deliciously cold. In its lower course the stream becomes salt, and does no good to any one. Farther on, we came to a river-bed, with some water; this river also becomes salt, but its course is to the plain of Rafsinjan. The hills now began to show colours, in some places of extraordinary brilliancy, red and rich brown, and mauve; and when we reached God-i-Ahmar, we found it a hollow surrounded by red hills. Here a pleasure-house had been built by one Ismail Khan, some time a great man in Rafsinjan and Pariz; but he had died twelve years ago, and his sons were wasting the property, as is usual. The eldest, Husain Khan, is still Zabit of the whole Pariz district. I heard no good of him. The pleasure-house has been neglected since Ismail's death; it was left unfinished, and is now beginning to want repair. It is on a most extensive scale, with rooms enough to lodge fifty people, with an *andarun* for the women, a bath, and a capital orchard and garden. The gardener lamented the good days of Ismail Khan, who used to come up here every summer. Husain Khan has never been near the place. I was supplied with excellent vegetables from the garden, including lettuces raised from English seed. I also had a good bathe in the *hammam*, which Sayyid Ali got warmed for me. There are four or five peasants' houses at God-i-Ahmar, and a little cultivation watered by a qanat. Outside the house I found an encampment of donkeys. They were carrying cotton to Rafsinjan. On the march we had met a man with three ass-loads of piece-goods, which he was taking for sale in the little hamlets scattered among the hills. Thus are the goods of Manchester distributed over the farthest corners of the East.

In the evening I went to the top of a hill above God-i-Ahmar, and enjoyed the view till the light failed. The air was clear and cold. A waste of hills lay all around, dark and formless, save towards the east, where two high peaks, all white with snow, rose over the road, and to the far north-west, where the mountains of Maimanda could just be seen, white against the horizon.

9th April, Bahramabad, 8 farsakhs; 8 a.m. to 5 p.m.—We had eight farsakhs to march next day. The road descends the bed of the river, winding among the mountain-tops, and passes three villages at twelve, fourteen, and sixteen miles from God-i-Ahmar. At the last village we breakfasted, overlooking the Rafsinjan plain, which was simmering and shimmering in the hot air. The rest of the march was one long descent towards Bahramabad—a descent like riding into a misty region of fairyland. We rode down, down, through the dreamy afternoon, surrounded by mocking mirages, towards houses and orchards that swayed and danced above the ground. Even the high sun, involved in the haze born of his own beams, seemed like "a dragon's eye that feels the stress of a bedimming sleep." It was a long sixteen miles to Bahramabad. We sought quarters in the Persian telegraph-office, but it was too small, so we took the post-house (*chaparkhana*) instead. This had a small upper room, where I found satisfactory accommodation.

Bahramabad has prospered much of late years, on account of the increased trade between Yazd and Karman. It is well supplied with qanats, and has a watercourse running through it. There is a covered bazar, inferior to that of Saidabad. Cotton seems to be a great staple here. The telegraph is managed by a Shahzada, on eight tomans a month, who invited me to tea and a qalyan in the evening. He is a man of some education, of a contented mind, and of singularly subdued and deferential manners. In Teheran he had learned a few French and English phrases. Like all Persians who ever spoke to me on the subject, he had found French much easier than English. His Persian was choice and elegant. I learned from him something about Persian lines of telegraph. The line to Mashhad was completed a few years ago. The original estimates were so large that the Shah abandoned the project, but one of the Europeans in his service offered to construct the line at a much smaller cost, and did so successfully, in spite of the prevailing terror of the Turkomans. The line between Karman and Yazd was made last year by

Colonel Schindler of the Shah's service; I heard a good deal about him in Karman. This line goes on from Yazd to Isfahan. The Dizful and Shustar line is a year or two older. There was much difficulty, at first, in keeping up the line through Mazandaran. Snow, heavy rain, and forest-boughs were continually breaking it, and repairs were impossible while the roads held mud enough to swallow up horse and man ; so, on the whole, the telegraph used to work only two or three days per fortnight ; and, being judged not worth the trouble of maintenance, it was taken down. But it has been reconstructed; I saw it myself on my way to the Caspian.

10th April, Kabutar Khan, 7 farsakhs ; 8 a.m. to 4.30 p.m.—Karman was now three stages to the east of us. They are three monotonous stages, over the Rafsinjan plain, with the Dawiran mountains on the left hand, and the mountains of Pariz and Saadatabad on the right. The plain is about thirty miles broad, and rises slowly towards Karman, Bahramabad being 4700 feet above the sea, Kabutar Khan 5100, and Karman 5500. The plain is a bare expanse of hard clay, covered with small splinters of black stone, and looking not unlike a coke pavement on a clay soil. It is proverbially dry; the Shahzada quoted a proverb that says, "The packsaddle of a Rafsinjan ass is never wet" (*pálán i khar i Rafsinjan tar na mishavad*); but we were to see it under quite other conditions. Dawiran had a little snow, fallen two days before; the Maimand mountains and a couple of peaks of the Pariz mountains on our right were white all over; and Jupa before us, and Kala-i-gav (cow's head) on our right front, presented magnificent snowy masses in the distance. Behind us stretched the plain, far as one could see. For the first half of the march to Kabutar Khan villages were to be seen, at intervals of a few miles, on either hand; after that, mere plain, herbless, lifeless, save for little stone-coloured lizards with erect tails and large flat heads. Eighteen miles from Bahramabad is a shelterhouse with an abambar, where we breakfasted. The rest of our way was involved in a storm of wind, dust, and rain from the southwest. The tyranny of the wind is unchecked over these shelterless plains. Kabutar Khan has a good caravansarai, newly built of stone. We went to the chaparkhana, where the upper room had no doors, and was consequently uninhabitable during so high a wind. I had to occupy the one spare room downstairs, while Sayyid Ali took refuge with the family of the master of the chaparkhana.

11th April, Baghin, 8 farsakhs; 8.30 *a.m.* to 6 *p.m.*—Our next march was one of nine farsakhs, to Baghin. It had rained in the night, and the plain was partly under water. We had to leave the main road and keep to the skirts of the southern hills. After twenty miles, we found ourselves opposite a small village called Daulatabad. Here we were overtaken by a storm of wind and rain, which came up from the south-west with a certain grandeur, overshadowing the mountain-tops, and involving the plain in blackness. We fled to Daulatabad, over flooded stretches of slippery clay. A stream flowed between us and the village; we scrambled up and down its clay banks, and entered Daulatabad—the Abode of Wealth—a place which sadly belied its name. Ruined and empty mud-houses were all we saw, except, indeed, a cow or two. Zaki Beg's venerable charger stood disconsolate before a tottering gateway, with hanging head and rump turned to the wind and rain. Presently part of one side of the gateway came down with a run, and shrill female voices from within proclaimed that

Zaki Beg had invaded the sanctity of some domestic hearth. Sayyid Ali's persuasive powers, which are considerable, allayed the tumult, and I was invited under a large archway, with two rooms opening off the back. Here were three women spinning, and two men, and a couple of children, for whom Sayyid Ali produced sugar-cheese, purchased in Bahramabad. The women found bread, walnuts, and raisins for me, but had neither buttermilk nor curds. There was only one other inhabited house in the place. In half an hour the rain passed away, but we were overtaken by another wind-storm before reaching Baghin. I walked six of the nine farsakhs, and arrived tired and hungry. The chaparkhana was a ruin, so we went to a fine caravansarai of stone, just outside the village. Baghin is a large village, surrounded by the orchards which give it its name; but its present condition is one of dilapidation and decay.

12th April, Karman, 6 farsakhs; 7 a.m. to 3 p.m.—The Jupa Mountains, with their snowy summits 13,000 feet high, were a noble mark on our right, as we marched next day to Karman. We crossed the slopes of the northern hills, rising some sixty feet above the plain, and after eight miles we caught sight of Karman, fourteen miles away, a green expanse of trees, backed by high dark mountains, streaked with snow above. The approach to the city lay through muddy lanes, flooded and slippery; it was the vilest marching. In drizzling rain we entered Karman. The soldiers in the gate presented arms; we rode up the vacant street, and found our way to the telegraph office. Here was no accommodation, so passing through the bazar we sought the principal caravansarai, and hired two good upper rooms. I was glad to have reached a large city, where we could refit, and where some reasonable intelligence might be looked for regarding the country which lay between us and Yazd.

CHAPTER X.

KARMAN.

12TH TO 17TH APRIL.

ZAKI BEG went to the Governor's and returned with the kadkhudabashi, or Mayor of Karman, to whom was assigned the duty of ministering to our necessities. We were offered a change of quarters, but I preferred the caravansarai. For two days I rested and wrote letters; then I went out and called on the kadkhudabashi, who received me with much deference, gave me sherbet and a qalyan, and some information about Karman. After a while he offered me wine, which I accepted with thanks. It was light *vin ordinaire*, but he had better stuff in his cellars, for Sayyid Ali next day brought me a great *baqqâra* or glass vessel, containing about three quarts of dark strong wine, which he had purchased from the kadkhudabashi for five krans. This wine was so strong that I had to mix it with water. Moreover, Sayyid Ali bought six bottles of brandy, three for himself and three for me, at three and a half krans per bottle—a magnificent bargain, for the brandy proved to be very fair. It had come from Bombay to a trader of Karman, who finding no market for it in the city, was glad of this opportunity of getting it off his hands.

Next day I called on the Vazir, who gets the credit of governing the whole province. I found him a comparatively young man, with a reddish nose of ultra-Persian dimensions; for the rest, he spoke in a quiet tone of voice, and was extremely civil. The room in which we sat was adorned with the usual tawdry pictures taken from bundles of piece-goods, and set in the fair white plaster of the wall, alternating with small mirrors similarly set, which make a better show. We talked of the assassination of the Emperor of Russia—an astounding piece of news which I heard here for the first time. "There are Nihilists in all countries," said the Vazir; "we have our Nihilists in Persia, whom we call Bâbis." At a subsequent interview, I tried to get news of our doings in Afghanistan, and of the Russians in the Turkoman country; but the Vazir had nothing to tell me, save that the Biluchistan mail would be in next day, and that he would send me anything of interest which it might contain. I never saw it; but l succeeded in procuring some copies of the *Akhtar*, a Persian newspaper published in Constantinople, which, though old, were better than nothing.

The Prince Governor (Farman Farma) of Karman, having appointed an evening for my visit, I went to the palace, and was ushered into a large plainly-furnished room, opening on a courtyard with plane-trees and apple-trees, and with three small fountains prettily playing. A broad divan, covered with red cloth, occupied part of one side of the room, and beside it, on a high bedstead, sat the prince. He is very like his brother the then Governor of Shiraz, but older and feebler. He was enveloped in a great fur cloak. His manners were courteous and calculated to set one at one's ease. Having visited Europe with the Shah in 1873, he has much in common with Europeans, and there need be none of those appalling gaps and flaws in the conversation which render an Indian *mulaqat* so peculiarly fearful. He asked about the fate of Candahar, and could scarcely believe that it was to be given up, after the expenditure of so much blood and treasure. He politely acquiesed, however, in my suggestion that Candahar was of no use to us. Speaking of India, he told me he had heard of the Naini Tal landslip, and proceeded to explain the same to his physician in an erroneous fashion, which I did not consider myself called on to correct. He had lately been marching in the high mountain country to the east of my route from Forg to Saidabad, in the hope of getting rid of his gout, and had actually derived seme benefit from the excursion, besides seeing what he described as a charming country. "Six marches from Karman," he said, "there is a defile of stupendous and awful depth, opening on a lovely country of woods and waterfalls—a fairyland which if Farangis could behold, they would desert their Naini Tal, and build there." I doubt it. Finally, the prince lamented that he had the gout, and, pulling off his stocking, showed me his gouty toe. I know not if this was done in order that I might be able to give the lie to the popular rumour which represents the prince's malady as a gangrene—a disease which is attributed, probably without reason, to the royal family in general. The present case was clearly one of gout. I had half a mind to make the prince a present of a bottle of chlorodyne, to give him sleep towards morning, when his toe is most troublesome; but on consideration I found I had none to spare. After tea, coffee, and qalyans, I took my leave, much pleased with the gentlemanly affability of the Farman Farma. "A qalyan isn't a bad thing," he said, as he smoked with a relish. I noticed that my qalyan had a tiny paper picture of the Madonna and Child set in the gold, rubies, and turquoises which embellished its top.

Karman city is about a mile long from north to south, and three-quarters of a mile broad from east to west. It is enclosed by a mud wall, in good preservation, with six gates, and with a ditch which is partly filled up. About one-seventh of the city is outside the walls. Architectural monuments there are none. Yet the city is ancient; its site has been marked out by Nature for the habitation of men since the beginning of ages; and certain relics of antiquity remain, though mean and ruined. The Qubba-i-Sabz, or Green Cupola, is the most commanding object in Karman, and catches the eye as the first glimpse of the city presents itself across the grey plain, fourteen miles away. To those accustomed to Oriental ideas of colour, it will cause no surprise to learn that the colour of the Green Cupola is blue. It is a strange cylindrical structure, covered by a dome; the height is about forty feet, and the diameter of the tower about thirty feet. The domed roof, covered with blue tiles, remains entire, and traces are visible on the interior of blue-tiled wainscoting and floral and starry designs painted on white plaster, and indeed the blue-and-gold frescoes of the ceiling are hardly faded; but great gaps and fissures deface the walls, which, though exceeding thick, are built of no costlier stuff than half-baked bricks of clay. In the middle of the floor is a marble tomb, chipped and worn; while high on the wall, too high to be legible, is a small *tughra* inscription, giving the date and the builder's name. For want of a ladder these must remain unknown. The building is said to be 700 years old. A modern inscription records the fact that straw was stored here for the army of Jaafar Ali Khan, in 1273 of the Hegira—twenty-five years ago. The people say, of course, that the dome was filled with straw to the very top. As for other buildings, the Jami Masjid or chief mosque is scarcely distinguishable from the mud-plastered houses around. Dome and minaret, those invariable features of the Indian mosque, are usually wanting in Persia, and the sacred character of the edifice is often revealed only by its gaily-tiled door. But the Karman tiles have little better to show than conventional arrangements in blue, white, and green; and only one building recalls, and that distantly, the lavish and lovely flower-patterns which adorn so many old walls and gateways in Shiraz. This building is the Madrasa of Ibrahim Khan, a court-yard surrounded by two-storeyed apartments, not high, but well-built of stone, with bright and variegated faces reflected in the tank in the centre. Some show of learning is maintained here, and as the rooms of the mullahs are well-carpeted and neat, and the Mujtahid's house extremely comfortable with its green jalousies, I presume the property left in trust for the college is administered with tolerable fidelity. An older Madrasa is that called the Masumia; it is narrow, gloomy, and heavily built of stone. But perhaps the oldest building in or about Karman is the ruined mud fort attributed to Ardshir, which stands on two steep hills of limestone, about 100 feet high, half a mile north-west of the city. The walls line the face of the hill, and some of the towers still stand thirty feet high from the off-set of their foundations on the steep white slope.

They are built of unbaked bricks, two feet square by nine inches thick in the lower courses. In this climate clay lasts like stone. A few small vaulted rooms keep their roofs yet. One gets a good view of the city from the ruined battlements, which were swept, when I visited them, by an ear-piercing wind, shrill, chill, with puffs of dust. Old Karman can be seen south of the city, an area of low mud ruins. Agha Muhammad Khan is believed to have laid it waste, and to have shifted Karman to its present site. To the west, under a black hill, are some ruins surrounding a domed edifice said to have been a fire-temple destroyed by Ali. A few gardens brighten the view in this direction; but Karman is not nearly so rich in gardens as Shiraz.

Shah Niamat Khan, the holy man of Mahun (a mountain village one day's march to the south-west), who lived a hundred years ago, and "gave information," as the Persians say, "of a thousand years before and a thousand years after," and who, moreover, foretold or foreshadowed in some fashion the Indian Mutiny—has prophesied that the three chief cities of Persia shall be destroyed as follows:— Isfahan by water, Yazd by sand, and Karman by horses' hoofs. Some morning the people of Karman shall wake and see the Saidi hills, north of the city, all white with tents; and then they will know that the end has come, that the rule of the Qajars, as my guide observed with joy, is over and done with. Whence the new conqueror is to come, the holy man has not stated; but it appears that the water which shall engulf Isfahan has its source in the Karman hills. In the reign of Nadir Shah, a shepherd in the Kuh Payah, that lofty and irregular mountain mass which forms a dark background to the northern walls of Karman, lost a goat, which had wandered into a cleft of the rock. He followed, striking the sides of the cavern with his stick in the darkness. On a sudden, in answer to a random blow, a stream of water burst from the rock, and swept him off his feet and out of the cave, snatching his stick also out of his hand. This was a grave loss, for the stick, like that detected by Sancho Panza, was hollow, and contained a store of coins. Some time after, the shepherd had occasion to go to Isfahan, and in the shop of an old rag-merchant (*simsâr* or *qarrâzi*) he saw his well-known stick. He bought it for a trifle, opened it, and found his money. The shopkeeper now claimed the stick as his own, and the quarrel came before the king. It was proved that a man had picked the stick out of the Zaindarud river, in Isfahan, and had disposed of it to the rag-merchant. The water struck by the shepherd out of the mountain above Karman had carried the stick all the way to Isfahan. Nadir Shah at once marched to Karman, and had the mouth of the cave built up in his presence, and there the water is bottled up to this day; but when the hour comes it will escape, and wash Isfahan into the sea.[1] Concerning which story it may be remarked that any water starting from Karman for Isfahan would find its resting-place in the low levels of Yazd, half-way between the two cities.

Ardshir's fort has also a story attached to it. That monarch, or one of his successors, wished to make his daughter marry somebody she had not a mind to. She shut herself up in the fort, and sustained a siege of twelve years, till a wise man passed that way and advised the king to stop the qanat which supplied water to the fort; whereupon the young lady surrendered,

[1] This story about the shepherd and his staff is not the peculiar property of Karman. I heard it told also of a mountain above Qum.

but whether she married her objectionable lover or not, I was unable to discover. There is a well (they say) in this fort, which has subterranean communication with the plain of Rafsinjan: I did not see the well, and in fact it is said to be filled up.

When General Goldsmid and the Perso-Baluch frontier mission visited Karman ten years ago, they were welcomed by the Vakil-ul-Mulk, or Vicegerent, then governing in the room of his deceased father, whose able administration had done so much for the prosperity of Karman. The title is now extinct, and the family are ruined. On the death of the Vakil-ul-Mulk, his property was confiscated or despoiled, and the province passed into the hands of the present Prince Governor, who was the Vakil's father-in-law. The memory of the old Vakil is still cherished in Karman. It was he who built the greater part of the covered bazar, as also the caravansarai where I lodged. This is one of the best I have seen in Persia. A space sixty yards square is surrounded by two-storied ranges of buildings, containing rooms which, if small, are clean, comfortable, and in good repair. The flooring of the courtyard, of the rooms, and of the broad balcony before the upper rows of rooms, consists of red tiles neatly laid. In the courtyard are two tanks of clean water. The gates in two sides of the square, opening into the bazar, are adorned with blue and yellow tiles; and one of them has two minarets, like square Italian towers, rising about sixty feet high, and by no means devoid of grace. In one tower is a clock, which keeps Persian time, counting from sunset to noon, and from noon to sunset. On the whole, I considered myself as very well off in the caravan-sarai, though the curiosity of the people was rather troublesome at first. They told me of another Farangi who was living on the opposite side. I went round to see him. He proved to be a Greek of Smyrna, who knew no language except Greek, Turkish of Constantinople, and a little Portuguese, so it was hopeless to try to cultivate his acquaintance. With him was a Turk who spoke Persian and acted as interpreter. The business of the Greek was to sell piece-goods and buy carpets. He had been there seven months, and seemed to be doing pretty well. Karman, as every one knows, is famous for its manufacture of carpets. I went to see a factory, reputed to be the largest in the city, though employing less than thirty hands. The wretched weavers sat in two low rooms, filled with a sour and sickening atmosphere. Most of them were pale-faced, weakly children of ten or twelve years, who hardly looked up as I entered, but remained bent over their work, picking up the threads with their nails, which are kept long, and notched for the purpose. The patterns are written out in pamphlets, and painfully committed to memory, and the children are taught very young—the younger the better. Their memories are quicker than those of grown-up folk. So far as I could understand the patterns, they seemed to be written in much the same style as those directions for knitting or crochet which one sometimes finds on a lady's table—*knit two, purl one, thread over, and knit two together.* There was also a youth employed in reading one of the patterns aloud. I am utterly destitute of taste in carpets, and gladly made my escape; nor had I the courage to enter a shawl manufactory to which I was next conducted. A carpet about sixteen feet by ten can be purchased in Karman for forty to fifty tomans— say 16*l.* to 20*l.* Some carpets take a year to make, and a decently-good carpet will not be finished in less than three months; thus, although there are several hundred factories in and about Karman, the outturn of carpets is in no way alarming. The Persians themselves prefer Manchester rugs, hideous things bearing the portraiture of a camel or a lion, Bay of Naples, Leaning Tower of Pisa, and the like.

There is room for other and more valuable manufactures in Karman, if the Government possessed enlightenment and integrity. Coming through the mountains of Pariz, I was struck with the highly metallic appearance of the rocks in places. It seemed to me that the hills must be full of iron. I heard vague tales of mines, but in Karman I got authentic information from a Persian master-miner. This was a spare, hungry-eyed man, an enthusiast who had made little by his profession, but had evidently acquired much practical skill and an extensive acquaintance with the mineral districts about Karman. He showed me specimens of lead and copper ores from a place called Tang-i-Mor-i-Aspan, or Horse-grass Pass, distant four farsakhs from Pariz and two from God-i-Ahmar. The ores seemed very rich. The Persian Government, however, wants only mines of the precious metals or of precious stones. They gave the miner eight workmen, and ordered him to find a silver mine in the mountains above Karman. He sunk a shaft fifty feet deep, and struck lead, whence he proposed to extract silver. But the Government could not wait, and bade him find, if not silver, at least turquoises. He did so, and sent two boxes of turquoises to Teheran, paying the carriage ; and has heard nothing more about them. He showed me specimens of his turquoises in the rough. There were four kinds of copper ore, he said: blue-soil (*lil-bum*), violet (*banafsha*), green, and red ; the two former being the best. Coal also is found in Deh Taki, six farsakhs north of Karman, and is brought into the city for sale in the winter. Perhaps, however, this coal (*zughál i sang*) is merely anthracite. When Mr. Blanford was in Karman, ten years ago, he was taken to visit coal-diggings near Karman, which produced only anthracite of an inferior description. However this may be, doubtless the mountains of Karman contain minerals in plenty, which an energetic Government might work with profit. After laying the Yazd-Karman telegraph line, Colonel Schindler made a tour in these parts, collecting specimens. My miner was with him. " One day," said he, " we were in Pariz together, and the Sartip asked me what there was remarkable in the neighbourhood. I told him that at Faridun, two farsakhs distant, there was an ancient avenue of chinars (plane-trees), and an old graveyard with inscriptions on the tombs in a character which nobody could read." The poor man was anxious that I should take him with me on a similar cruise; but my plans were otherwise.

The Hindoos of Karman came to pay me their respects. They are about forty souls, all from Shikarpur, and mostly in the service of two seths or bankers of that place, but a few have come over on their own account. The youngest of the community has been fourteen years in Persia. They represented their life in this strange land as a wretched one, but did not seem at all keen to return to India. In their Persian dress and tall felt hats they presented a miserable contrast to the genuine Persian. I never was more forcibly reminded of the physical inferiority of the Hindoo race. They looked like withered black apes. In the evening I went to see them in their caravansarai, called that of the Hindoos; it belongs to the Qazi of the city, whose patronage is useful to them. One of their number had died that morning, and I had noticed a crowd in the bazaar, as I rode by, waiting to behold the funeral; a tree also had been pointed out to me, beyond the walls, called the Hindoo-burning plane-tree (*Chinar i Hindu-suz*), where the body was to be burned. Four farrashes attended the funeral, and received two krans each, and their naib or sergeant had two more, such being the customary fee. The farrashbashi, however, who is the head of all the noble company of farrashes, demanded two tomans for himself. The Hindoos protested, and tried to telegraph to the British Minister at Teheran, but the telegraph clerk referred the matter to the Prince Governor. Affairs stood thus when I made my visit. The Hindoos professed to be in a lamentable state, but seemed comfortable enough, and when the farrashbashi came to negotiate a compromise, they let him know their mind fearlessly in choice Persian slang. Perhaps my presence encouraged them, though I gave them to understand distinctly that I had no intention of interfering; and so came away. At night, as I was finishing my dinner, in walked the Hindoos again, with tidings of victory. The Prince Governor had sent for them, had summoned the farrashbashi, abused him, and made him pay up part of twenty-one tomans which he had extorted from them on previous occasions; and the farrash-bashi had subsequently fled to avoid further proceedings. Moreover, the Vazir had called the Hindoos to him as they left the Prince, and had told them to apply to him always in similar cases. He was ashamed, no doubt, of the Prince's interference over his head. Thus the Hindoos triumphed, as I had expected. They did not seem to me to be much oppressed. They are not allowed to have a temple, or to worship in public; but they keep a private chapel in the house of their principal man. Their trade is with Karachi and Bombay; payments are made by bills on Bandar-Abbas, or gold is even remitted by courier (*qâsid*) to Bandar-Abbas—a fact which says a good deal for the safety of the roads.

More interesting than these traders was a Hindoo fakir, who came in, as I thought, to beg; but he assured me that he wanted no alms, merely a little intellectual conversation. He was a native of Firuzabad town in the Agra district, a Brahmin by caste, had left his home in youth, and followed his Guru or spiritual master to Cabul, where he lived twelve years, and thence, on his Guru's death, went to Herat. This place he seemed to like best of all; there is (or was) a large Hindoo community, with a temple, near which he built a small shrine of his own and lived happily. While he was there the Heratis were constantly fighting with the Turkomans. He left Herat five years ago, and returned to India, gravitated again towards Afghanistan when the war broke out, and was in Candahar during its siege (*qala'bandi*) by Ayub Khan. Returning to Karachi, he sailed for Bandar-Abbas, and came up to Karman. He was a wanderer on the face of the earth; the passion of travel had seized him, and he could find no rest for the sole of his foot. He told me that Indian piece-goods and tea found their way to Herat; also turmeric and coarse and fine sugar.

On our first arrival in Rafsinjan we had heard rumours of a bread famine in Karman, of negligence or incompetence on the part of the Prince Governor, and mismanagement on the part of the Vazir. In Karman itself we saw the bakers' shops beset by small crowds, betokening some difficulty in getting bread. It would be hard to say what caused the hitch. Rafsinjan had suffered from drought, but the city seemed to be well enough supplied, and perhaps the high prices were due to manipulation of the grain market for the benefit of those in power. The day after our arrival the Prince Governor cut off the ears and plucked out the beard of a baker in the bazar. My servants had no difficulty in buying as much bread as we wanted. On the whole, Karman appeared eminently quiet and peaceful after experience of Fars. Here were no tufangchis, but regular soldiers in shabby blue tunics and trousers, with old muzzle-loading muskets and rifles, rusty bayonets, and most imperfect notions of drill. They saluted me whenever I passed, and looked as little unsoldierlike as they could. Poor souls, they get indifferent pay at long intervals, and have to subsist mainly as artisans and hangers-on of the bazaar. I wished to see the artillery, but was told that the arsenal (*qûrkhana*) had been damaged by the rain, and was all in confusion. This was the second time that I had been unable to get into a Persian arsenal. The reason may have been jealousy, or it may have been shame to show an European such poor warlike preparations. It is but justice to the Persians to say that jealousy and exclusiveness towards foreigners are not a marked trait of the national character.

Of the merchants and trade of Karman I saw

little. Rafsinjan produces cotton, which is cultivated with great care; the field is dug over, then trodden by cattle, and finally the pulverized earth is rammed flat with wooden mallets. I did not see much poppy in Rafsinjan. The direct route to Bandar-Abbas seems to be gaining favour of late years. In the Karman post-office (where I watched the distribution of letters, and was rather impressed with the business-like character of the performance) I found a map of this route, but could not make it tally with my information picked up in Sirjan. It is creditable to the Government that the route is quite safe, and perhaps, if its development proceeds, the consequences may be very beneficial both to Karman and Bandar-Abbas. By this route come China tea and Manchester piece-goods from India, also Indian spices, and sugar mostly from Mauritius. Compared with this, the trade by the northern routes from Russia is but small. It consists chiefly of *khurda-farush* or pedlar's wares, as cutlery, candlesticks, tea-cups (made of glass), small mirrors, and things of that sort. Some of the shopkeepers, however, assured me that the best tea came from Astrachan, caravan-borne *viâ* Orenburg; if so, it is a marvellous round.

Fortunes are to be made by trade in Rafsinjan as elsewhere. In Bahramabad I had heard of a pedlar named Khwaja Ali who from small beginnings had amassed great wealth, without, however, making any change in his humble style of life; marching over the plain, I had crossed kanats which he was making; and here, in Karman, I found him building a caravansarai. What a contrast to Husain Khan, son of the late magnificent Ismail! In Karman they told me Husain's profession was mere *lutigiri* or blackguardism; he was in arrears with his revenue, and had to mortgage three villages. This caravansarai of Khwaja Ali's is the seventh in the city of Karman. Two of them are called after the Zardashtis and Hindoos respectively. The Zardashtis or Zoroastrians are fire-worshippers, called also Gabrs. They have their separate quarter, where the women go about unveiled, with long plaited hair.

In Karman I made some changes in my establishment. One of my two horses had a frightful sore back; I sold him and bought a pony and a horse of mature years, of extraordinary woebegone and cadaverous appearance, and a fine development of bone. This animal was fondly expected to put on flesh and become creditable under the fostering care of my groom —a perfectly worthless youth, whom, nevertheless, I retained for want of a better. No words can do justice to the bad qualities of Persian servants. They are lazy, thievish, careless, dirty, without one spark of interest in their work or affection for their master. I remember reading Colonel MacGregor's account of Persian servants, how he tried one, then two together, then three, and always found them useless. I thought the colonel must be in the wrong, but shortly after landing in Persia I began to find him entirely in the right. Let me, however, exempt one of my servants from the imputation of thieving,—viz., the lad Husain, whom I picked up in Karman. I had now three servants, a cook, a groom, and Husain for general inefficiency. The Prince Governor had also given me a ghulam, so our caravan now consisted of nine men, five horses, and five mules.

CHAPTER XI.

KARMAN TO YAZD.

SEVENTY-THREE FARSAKHS: THIRTEEN DAYS.

FROM Karman to Yazd, one has the choice of two routes. A range of mountains—the Kuh Dâwirân—extends between the two places; Karman being at one end of the chain, and Yazd at the other. On either side of this central chain is a parallel range; and the traveller from Karman may follow either the valley on the right side of the central chain, or that on the left. The latter (Rafsinjan) is somewhat the larger of the two, is better peopled, has the telegraph, and is the grand highway of commerce. The right-hand valley (Zarand) was that by which I wished to travel; but instead of taking the main road up the centre of the valley, which is level clay and salt, I kept along its northern edge, on the slopes at the foot of the mountains, some few hundred feet higher. These mountains are marked on the map as Kuh Nugat, but I found no recognition of that name in the villages at their feet. The mountains, as usual, have particular names from the villages which they overshadow; and as for the whole range in general, the only name I could discover was the Kuh-i-Hutkan. My purpose was to get behind the range into the reputed "fertile highlands" of Kuhbanan, which I pictured to myself as an extensive, well-cultivated plateau.

18*th April, Sar Asiab*, 6 *farsakhs* ; 7.30 *a.m. to* 3 *p.m.*—Our first day's march was to Sar Asiab, or Mill-Head. The road passes the western end of the Saidi hills, on a spur of which, a mile to the right and two miles outside the city, is the tower where the fire-worshippers expose their dead (*dakhma-i-Gabrhâ*). Soon after, limestone hills begin to appear on the left, at first in isolated peaks, the largest being the Maiden's Fort (a common name for rock-forts in Persia), a naturally-scarped eminence some 300 feet high, with remains of fortifications on the summit, and traces of a winding path to the top. At ten miles the limestone hills become continuous, and the road ascends between them and the Hutkan range, now drawing nearer on the right. Crossing the long undulations of its foot-slopes, we came at last in sight of the orchards of Sar Asiab. A noble chinar stands over the village qanat, before the door of the caravansarai, a new stone building, clean and solid, but without a keeper. We preferred to seek shelter in the village, and found good quarters in the kadkhuda's house. Here, for the first time, I received *sursât* or gratuitous purveyance of provisions, much against my will. The ghulam Sayyid, whom the Prince Governor had deputed to accompany me, was a native of Azarbaijan, spoke Persian with a strong Turkish accent, and had a large contempt for the people of Karman. Moreover, the Prince Governor had given me a letter in which sursât was distinctly mentioned as my right; so the hapless kadkhuda of Sar Asiab had to feed me and my people for nothing. Of course he laid the village under contribution. I was slightly unwell (the result of careless eating in Karman), and shirked the question by going to sleep. It was satisfactory, at any rate, that the kadkhuda made no complaint.

19th April, Khanuk, 6 farsakhs ; 7 a.m. to 2.30 p.m.—Next day we marched under the Hutkan range, which rose 1500 to 2000 feet above us on our right. The long grey slope at its foot is neither verdant nor well-watered, but mere shelves and ridges of hard clay mixed with stones, and sometimes dotted with camel-thorn; but in nooks and bays formed by spurs of the hills, or in the mouth of ravines discharging a slender stream, little villages find means to sustain themselves, and make the rocks bright with foliage of fruit-trees and emerald patches of wheat. These are tiny hamlets, sometimes perched up in the rocks; but on the slope itself stand three larger villages, watered by qanats, between Sar Asiab and Khanuk. We marched through all three, and noticed the new cultivation of the poppy. Then we crossed a little spur of the mountains, and came down on Khanuk. It is a flat-roofed stone-built village, with a ruined mud fort on a mound in the centre, and with fine orchards around. My quarters were under an archway open towards the courtyard where the whole caravan found room. The village was in great distress. Yesterday, after half an hour's rain, a torrent of mud, stones, and water had come down from the mountains, and choked up and abolished the qanat on which the hopes of the harvest depend. The kadkhuda had gone to Karman, to try to induce the Government, which owns three-fourths of the village, to repair the damage. The cost was estimated at 250 tomans, or nearly 100*l*. In these circumstances, it was little wonder that the chief men of the village took occasion to ask me privately whether the *sursât* provided for us would be allowed for in the revenue collections. I told them that it was extremely doubtful, and called for an account. The whole bill came to only eight and a half krans (about seven shillings). I paid it, and thought the matter was settled. But in the morning Sayyid Ali and Sayyid ghulam discovered the fact, and began a pretty altercation with the villagers. It is not easy to decide what one should do in such cases. If one were able to protect the people, the simple and obvious course of paying for everything might be safely followed; but the traveller has to pass on, and the villagers are left exposed to the vengeance of petty officers, who consider their authority as insulted by any demand for payment. The chief men were so frightened that they returned the money, which of course I could not think of accepting. After rebuking Sayyid Ali and the ghulam, I settled the controversy by saying that the trifling sum was intended merely as a token of satisfaction and an acknowledgment of hospitality; and so went away, very doubtful whether I had not done more harm than good. Perhaps the *sursât* might have been allowed for in the revenue, after all.

20*th April, Zarand,* 5 *farsakhs ;* 7 *a.m. to noon.*—Leaving the village, we crossed the bed of the torrent which had wrought such damage. It came from a gorge two miles above Khanuk, where a little stream is expended in irrigating a little village. The rain on the mountains must have been something like a small waterspout, for the stream came down with abundant mud, and stones weighing half a hundredweight; it was thirty yards broad and four feet deep where it passed Khanuk, and it descended the slope about two miles before it spread out and lost itself in the stony soil. We were now descending into the plain, which we had seen from Sar Asiab and Khanuk, lying far below us on our left, with green villages scattered at long intervals over the white clay and gleaming salt, swept by whirling columns of dust. Two villages lay at the foot of the slope. We had an invitation to one of them from its owner, Sultan Khan, but it lay a mile out of our way, and as I was somewhat unwell, and impatient to reach Zarand, I went to the other village, and breakfasted there, then marched down the plain to Zarand, through dust and wind. We found good quarters in the empty house of one Ibrahim Khan. The governor of Zarand came to see me in the evening; also Sultan Khan, who regretted that I had not called at his village, where he had made preparations for my reception. It was indeed a defect of courtesy, for which I made excuse on the plea of indisposition. Zarand district contains about five-and-twenty villages, whereof fifteen are in the plain, and ten on the long slopes under the Hutkan mountains. The ways and means of Persian irrigation are very well exemplified in this district. The uppermost villages, or rather hamlets, situated in the mouth of clefts and gorges, draw their water from natural springs and brooks; these sink into the stony slope, and are tapped two miles lower down by the qanats of the larger villages below; finally, filtering through fifteen miles of slow descent, the waters reach the levels of the plain, and feed the qanats of the villages along the main road. Further across the plain there is no water. Under the Dawiran range lies a glittering strip of kavir. A solitary hill breaks the evenness of the plain; it is about 400 feet high, and has a shrine at the top, sacred to one Hayât Bibi, or Lady of Life, of whose history I was not able to discover anything.

21st April, Tughraja, 9 farsakhs; 7.30 *a.m.* to 6 *p.m.*—I rejoiced to know that our next march would carry us at last into the promised land behind the Hutkan range. Hitherto the mountains had sheltered only isolated villages, wherever a little river-bottom afforded width enough for cultivation; and if we had penetrated into this country, we must have carried our provisions with us; but now we were marching for the "fertile highlands" of Kuhbanan, where is a whole *baluk* or district with a governor of its own. We reascended the slope, and at sixteen miles reached a hamlet of two houses, where we breakfasted. Then, drawing obliquely nearer to the mountains, we crossed the neck of a long spur which they send out here into the plain. Behind the spur are two small plateaux, one after the other, both empty, but with good grazing for flocks. We could now see the high precipitous peak of the mountain at whose foot lay our halting-place, Tughraja, but we had yet to cross the valleys of three little streams which unite to form a river that descends into the Zarand plain and becomes salt. In these upper valleys their water is but slightly brackish, and it irrigates fair green fields, slopes clad with vineyards and orchards, and rows of plane-trees and willows by the side of lanes which seemed to me more English than anything I had seen in the East. The last part of the march was a long ascent. We had nearly ceased to believe in the existence of Tughraja, when we crossed the last saddle-back, and beheld an orchard at our feet. It was most picturesquely situated, covering an irregular patch of ground between two hills, and at the confluence of two ravines, so that the trees, overflowing the scanty level plot, hung upon the slopes, and straggled down the ravines, whose upper courses supplied the water-channels that ran sparkling under the green shade. Tughraja itself lay behind a hill on our left, overlooking a long plateau. Evidently we were now inside the Hutkan mountains, and this plateau must be some thousand feet higher than Zarand plain, while Tughraja village again stood three hundred feet above the plateau. On the farther side of the plateau rose a low range of hills, and over their tops could be seen the dark saw-line of Dawiran. This table-land, thought I, must be the "fertile highlands" of Kuhbanan; but indeed Kuhbanan was a day's march distant, and the plateau supports only two small villages on the Tughraja river, which crosses the level space, finds its way through the hills on the farther side, and descends into the Zarand plain, where it waters a few villages before becoming intolerably salt. In Tughraja its water is sweet and beautifully clear; it fills a qanat that sends little channels all over the village, while the stream itself flows behind the village, under a slope clothed with white-blossoming orchards. At the back of the spacious archway where I lodged was a window overlooking the slope. The sound of the stream lulled me to sleep at night. Tughraja, like all mountain-villages, is built of stone. The houses are in pretty good repair. Walnut and plane and willow and fruit-trees overshadow the stone walls of the lanes. It is a pity only that the stream shrinks almost to nothing in summer. There were complaints of drought, and indeed all Karman suffered pretty severely from drought last year, though less than Fars. Our guide on this march showed me bread made of green herbs, which he said had been the food of the poor people for many months.

22nd April, Kuhbanan, 7 farsakhs; 7 a.m. to 4 p.m.—Next day we reached the veritable

Kuhbanan. It was by no means the kind of place that I looked for. After a long ascent over stony ridges, between the plateau on the one hand and the central chain of Hutkan on the other, we halted by a very slender spring, and I had full leisure to admire Kuhbanan from a distance of twelve miles, while I was eating my breakfast. It is a plain with an area of perhaps a dozen square miles, backed by a semicircle of hills, and green with orchards and fields, too extensively interspersed with white patches of salt. Five villages stand in the plain, Kuhbanan itself being the chief; they are well watered, and cultivate more poppy than wheat. This crop came into fashion five years ago, and the present year has been singularly favourable to it, rain-water having supplied the place of irrigation. On the edge of the plain we passed a shrine with two magnificent plane-trees; thence it was an hour's march to Kuhbanan, which lies almost at the foot of the hills. The village is embosomed in mulberry trees, and maintains a small manufacture of silk. The governor came out to meet me—a Teheran official, dressed in black, of a spare habit of body, and timid manners; evidently discontented with his exile in this uncivilized place. He gave me good quarters in a vacant house, while the mules and horses were stabled in the neighbouring Husainia.

23rd April, Halt at Kuhbanan.—Here I halted one day, partly because the black mule had fallen lame, and partly for my own sake, to set my health right. I had indulged too freely in the good things of Karman, and had suffered for it ever since. In Kuhbanan I was able to get plenty of excellent milk, and by making that my sole diet for two days, and taking also a little medicine, I got over my difficulties satisfactorily. Kuhbanan itself presents few attractions. It has, however, a name in local history. When the Afghans, under Ashraf and Mahmud, marched from Karman on Isfahan,[1] a portion of their army seems to have taken this route. One Latif Shah was then governor of Kuhbanan; him they slew, and sacked the district. On a spur of the hill above Kuhbanan are the remains of an old fort, and a little lower, a mile from the village, stands a platform of hewn stone with two low towers above it, called the throne of Latif Shah. More interesting to an Anglo-Indian are the beds of *kankar* or nodular limestone which are

[1] In 1721.

found in the middle of the plain. The people say that it forms the substratum of the soil everywhere, and prevents the growth of good wheat. It is evident, anyhow, that wheat has been almost superseded by poppy. The Kuhbanan people are in a lamentable state of ignorance. They have never heard of England, and consider Russia as the Great Power of the universe.

24th April, Deh Ali, 5 farsakhs ; 7.30 a.m. to 3 p.m.—We passed several mills in beginning our march next day, and others were visible higher up the mountain-side. Leaving these on the right, we ascended among low hills and crossed a little watershed at the fifth mile. Below this lay a tract of small steep hills and tiny streams, giving water to half a dozen petty hamlets scattered along or near the road at intervals of two to four miles. In contrast with these, the mountain-village of Bidun hung on the side of a mountain five miles on our right. Under the crest were still some streaks of snow, and the green orchards of Bidun (about 7000 feet high) looked like a cool and happy nest where the summer heat, that dries the poor brooks among which we were wandering, could never venture to come. We crossed another ridge, and came in sight of

Deh Ali. It stands at the right or northern end of a plain some ten miles long. At the southern end is a village watered by a river, which descends from Kuhbanan and subsides here in salt. Half-way between this village and Deh Ali, a hamlet called Shuru or Brackish struggles to maintain itself on the edge of a white patch of kavir. Deh Ali is more fortunate in having a qanat, fed from a mountain twelve miles distant, on whose side can be seen the village of Bazhgun, pleasantly situated and green enough, but they say its water supply is uncertain. The whole male population of Deh Ali turned out to see the stranger. I was received outside the village by a crowd of fifty or sixty people, who returned my salutation, and bowed as I passed. They had had word of my coming from the governor of Kuhbanan. The kadkhuda's house afforded us very fair quarters, opening on a court-yard with vines and a tank. My room was a spacious archway, at the back of which flowed a stream from the qanat, somewhat brackish, but cold and full of small fish. Our drinking-water came from an abambar. Deh Ali is within four marches of Yazd, and its people seem to have picked up some elementary geographical information from the traders of that city. They had heard of Bombay. England they knew under the name of London; and they asked me whether London did not pay tribute to Rus and Rum, evidently regarding Russia, Turkey, and Persia as the three empires which divided the world between them. They have very respectable sheep in Deh Ali, which are nourished chiefly on wild rhubarb. The last two miles of our road were covered with wild rhubarb, as far as one could see on either hand. Persian rhubarb might take the place of Turkey rhubarb, if any care were given to its cultivation. But the people leave rhubarb alone, and eat the bulb of the hyacinth. This flower brightens these low hills with many a pretty spire of faint pink and white bells.

25th April, Shaitur, 2 farsakhs.—Our next march, to Shaitur, was a short one. We were to lay in provisions at a village half-way, whither Sayyid ghulam had gone before daybreak, with the emissary of the governor of Kuhbanan. When we arrived, however, about eight o'clock in the morning, we found nothing had been done. The whole male population had fled at the sight of Sayyid's hat with its official badge; all doors were shut, and hammering at them evoked only feminine whisperings.

My boy Husain, being helped up a wall, descended into an empty court-yard, and let us in. Sayyid Ali's persuasive powers soon tempted forth three or four women, with whom he entered into negotiations, while I admired the qanat-stream flowing through the courtyard, and the small tank swarming with small fish. These excellent women presently baked us twenty-five pounds of very good bread, like ship's biscuit, and brought me fresh milk, more than I could drink. Meanwhile Sayyid and the Kuhbanan man had been making inquisition for barley on behalf of the cattle, and found wheat instead, some forty pounds, which we loaded up. For none of these things was payment asked or offered; nobody seemed to suffer under any sense of injustice, and I thought it the best plan, on the whole, to let the two officials and the villagers arrange the matter between themselves. We did, however, pay for three fowls produced by three old women. In this unwonted scene of plenty, Zaki Beg, I regret to say, was tempted to depart from his integrity, and forcibly abstracted a fowl from an ancient dame. To judge from the appearance of the bird, it might have been her playmate in the days of her infancy; at least, she valued

it as an old friend, and pursued the robber with
outcries. Zaki Beg was condemned to pay, and
retired shamefacedly. By this time the men of
the village, having first sent in single scouts to
report on our proceedings, and having found
them to be quite according to law and order,
came dropping in by twos and threes, and were
deservedly chaffed. We parted with them on
good terms, and marched to Shaitur against a
high wind, like a bleak March wind at home.
Finding no resting-place in the village, we went
to the fort of the chief man of these parts. He
himself was at Bâfk; but we were admitted, and
made ourselves comfortable enough. In the
afternoon I walked to the top of a small hill,
and surveyed the long table-land with its north-
eastern side bounded by dark mountains, and
its south-western edge rising against the horizon,
and there, apparently, dropping down to the
Zarand plain. A dozen little villages occupy
its centre, between Deh Ali and Shaitur; they
are watered by brackish qanats, and shaded by
sinjad trees,[2] a kind of willow with a strong
sickly scent, and a fruit like small dates. The
trees were now in flower, and their heavy per-

[2] Possibly this is the tree called *ailantus*. I found
nobody in Persia who could tell me its European name.

fume could easily be detected at the distance of a mile. The brackish water, which the sinjad loves, prohibits the cultivation of poppy. Madder *(runask)* takes its place. It is cultivated with much care, and is exported to Bombay, and some to Khurasan. In a hamlet called Deh Kuchak, near Shaitur, I inspected the madder fields, and admired their neatness. Two men came out and invited me into the village, where I enjoyed a qalyan and a conversation with the elders. Was I a Russian? they asked; but one of the company knew the name of *Inglîs*, having travelled to Mecca *viâ* Bandar-Abbas in an English steamer. He had been much impressed by the forts of Aden. I was also questioned as to the relations of the Persian Government towards England, Russia, and Turkey. One man asked whether the Shah's new bride (of whom I had never heard before) was not an English princess. After half an hour's talk, we exchanged a friendly adieu, and I walked back to Shaitur, having discovered, among other things, that a Farangi had passed that way six years ago, taking notes.

26th April, Bafk, 10 *farsakhs;* 6 *a.m. to* 6 *p.m.*—We had ten farsakhs between us and Bafk, with no intermediate halting-place. From our high table-land, green enough to support sheep, we were to descend through the Hutkan range into the Zarand plain again, but here far north of Zarand, where the plain is mere barrenness, stones and sand. As we filed through the little street of Shaitur, we saw the tableland rising before us to the south-west in a gradual slope, which marked a long line against the horizon at eight miles; and beyond this line, as we knew, began the descent towards Bafk, but whether abrupt or gradual we could not tell. When we reached the summit of the ascent, a wonderful tangle of hills appeared below, with the road winding round their bases and among their ravines as best it could, now following a dry torrent-bed, now taking advantage of a broken ledge of rock along some steep hill-side. But what caught the eye at once, and diverted it from this maze of strangely shaped and coloured peaks, was the grand gateway in which the pass terminated. It stood out clear against the morning sky, a great gap in a wall of rock, through which could be seen, much farther away than we desired, the broad naked plain of Bafk, even then beginning to cover itself with the haze of heat, though the day was still so young. We soon lost sight of the plain, but the sunlit summits of the great portal remained in view throughout all the windings of the road. Our devious descent continued for an hour, when we came on a slender rill, of course brackish, and presently found it gather force enough to flood half a dozen tiny terrace-fields, each of a few square yards, and to water the sheep of three or four pastoral houses, or rather holes in the rock, where the women-folk were making butter, while the men had driven the flocks afield. Though much alarmed at my portentous presence, nevertheless the oldest female, risking life and what else she had most precious, sought to propitiate the strangers with offering (duly paid for) of milk and curds, fire for the necessary qalyan, and information regarding the road. Under a tamarisk-tree— sad sign of our descent towards a warmer clime —we made a frugal breakfast, and resumed our way to the gates, now only three miles distant. They did not belie their promise of grandeur. They are 400 feet high, the first 100 feet being a steep slope, the rest sheer wall of rock; their depth is a quarter of a mile, their breadth 200 yards. Nowhere have I seen cliffs so sheer and plumb; they are a veritable wall, and in parts bore all the whiteness of a plastered wall, defaced by weather-stains. But a less pleasing sight was the shimmering plain below, with its six-and-twenty hot miles to be traversed somehow between noon and even. At nine miles is a small water-tank. No other object marks the level waste till the eye rests on the far mountain-chain that limits the plain on the west. As we left the gates, my men discovered a number of flourishing villages not more than ten miles on our left front. There were houses and palm-groves and the verdure of fields, plain enough; only, as my maps marked nought but wilderness, I was fain to doubt my eyes; and indeed the whole thing proved to be mirage, conjured up from the dry bed and sandy sides of the torrent which discharges itself through the cleft from which we had just emerged. Before we reached the tank, the wind rose and lifted the sand, which came against my pith hat like rattling hail, while every gust threatened to whirl that precious article, not to be replaced, over the infinite leagues of the plain, beyond the reach of footman or horse. But patience carries one through most things, and as the sun was almost sinking we crossed a low sandy ridge, and attained the outskirts of Bafk. There was some difficulty in finding a house. The first we tried was a dismal ruin; and while my people were hunting for another, I accepted an invitation to go and see the governor, who was enjoying tea and a pipe in his court-yard, in the presence of a few friends, a fountain, and some mulberry trees. At my appearance, dismay and doubt depicted themselves on the general countenance; nor do I wonder, for a more grimy and travel-stained individual probably never entered those precincts before. I advanced nevertheless, and sat down beside the Khan, took the proffered qalyan and tea-cup, and began conversation. A grave, black-bearded personage asked me whether I had seen that famous fountain in London which transmutes copper coins into gold. It was discovered accidentally some time ago, by a shepherd who drank water from it in the hollow of his hand, having a copper ring on his finger, which ring, when he next looked at it, he found changed to pure gold. The fountain is now the property of the Government, and the source of London's wealth. I informed him that I had not seen this remarkable natural phenomenon, and indeed was not aware of its existence. Talking of local geography, I heard great praises of a place called Gudrun, half-way between Bafk and the Zarand district, on a table-

Bafk. 243

land between the Hutkan mountains and a short parallel range. The specialty of Gudrun is that it unites the products of a warm and a cold climate; chinars and walnuts with pomegranates, oranges, and lemons. Having learned these and other things, I went to the quarters in which my people were now installed, and had a dinner of bread and cocoa, with good fresh milk. My apartment was a great domed room, raised above the court-yard, and entirely open in that direction. Lying on my bed, I could look up to the stars, and watch Orion moving slowly past the arch of the wide portal. A muazzin was calling with loud voice through the stillness of the night; not content with glorifying God, he took to chanting prayers at great length. There is nothing like this sound for reminding the European traveller that he is an alien in an eastern land. I lay and listened, and looked at the stars.

27th April, halt at Bafk.—We halted here a day to lay in stores. The Khan invited me to a light early meal of mulberries and sweetmeats in a garden, and called upon me in the evening. He had been only a year in Bafk, and gave no very good account of the place. It is a town of some 3000 inhabitants, planted in the midst of a wide desolation. Ancient qanats supply it with brackish water, and it abounds in mulberry, pomegranate, and palm-trees, which fill the gardens that extend two miles to the north of the town and almost connect it with two little outlying hamlets. As we came over the low sandy ridge yesterday, the green gardens of Bafk, its wind-towers, and the domes of two pleasure-houses of past days, made a brave show of stateliness and prosperity. But Bafk is poverty-stricken and stagnant. No trade has taken root here, the town lies off the main road, and the dates which were its pride have been smitten by cold for the last four years. It is, however, very healthy. A doctor tried to get up a practice here, but had to give up in despair and go to Gudrun. An old mosque in the centre of the town deserves mention. It is built round a court-yard into which you descend by steps; the material is stone, and the narrow heavy solid style of the work bespeaks a considerable antiquity. Architectural grace there is none.

28th April, Khan-i-Panj, 5 farsakhs; 7.30 to 11.50 a.m.—Bafk is not a good place to get away from. If your destination be Karman, you have to cross nine farsakhs of desert to Gudrun, with uncertainty of finding stores when you get there; if Yazd, there are eighteen farsakhs between you and Fahraj—the nearest habitation of man in this direction. In all other directions the desert spaces are as broad, or broader, and the villages ultimately to be arrived at are still more incapable of provisioning a caravan. The point we were aiming at was Yazd. We took two days' provisions, and marched for Khan-i-Panj, over two miles of drifting sand, where the road is marked out by pillars, then over hard clay, and thence into the kavir. This kavir comes down the whole way from Zarand. I had seen it from Khanuk, a narrow strip under the Dawiran range; but it receives great accessions from the two rivers we had crossed in the hills on our way to Kuhbanan. We found it six miles broad, a perfectly level tract of salt-encrusted clay, dotted with thistles here and there, that looked as large as gooseberry bushes. In the middle is a salt stream, the unabsorbed remnant of the two united rivers; we crossed it by a ford paved with stones, all other places being impassable quagmire, as the guide said. Beyond the kavir, the plain grows hard and stony, and slopes upwards to Khan-i-Panj. Half-way are the ruins of a village which has succumbed to drought and isolation. The tamarisk trees watered by the old qanat still form a patch of green shade in the arid landscape. Khan-i-Panj consists of a stable and some small outhouses, little vaulted chambers, more like hen-houses than human habitations.[2] Hard by are two water-tanks of foul and brackish water, greasy, slightly sickening, overlying a deposit of stinking black mud. Sand-hills close the prospect on one side, kavir on the other; beyond the white salt bed of the river, the Hutkan range can be dimly seen through the warm air. We halted, put the animals under shelter, and disposed ourselves among the huts, seeking rest till the evening. Outside, the furious wind, which blows all day throughout the spring and summer, howled at its sweet will over salt and sand, and whirled about the straw left by the last caravan which had visited the place; for Khan-i-Panj is a mere shelter-house without inhabitants, and indeed it was

---

[2] There were workmen at the place a few days before making bricks and repairs. Sayyid Ali, searching for quarters, found none better than the brick-kiln, where he slept serenely. I read "Paradise Lost" till I should fall asleep, but Satan held me awake.

only by chance that we found a few sticks of fuel wherewith to cook our dinner. Towards evening, as the wind fell, we crept forth; it became possible to wash; and the sweet hour of dinner arrived for beasts and men.

28*th April, near Chah-Kavar*, 6 *farsakhs;* 6.30 *p.m. to* 1.30 *a.m. on* 29*th*.—An hour before sunset we were on the march again. Crossing the low sandy hills, we advanced into the desert and the shades of night, over a stony plain broken by long gentle waves, and bounded by ghostly mountain-shapes far away on either hand, half seen or guessed at in the uncertain light. We had coolness and calm, and the quiet light of the stars; it was pleasanter marching than under the midday sun, in the driving dust and gravel. "See," said one of the muleteers, "how the property marches in the cool night;" and indeed it was so. The mules stepped out at a good four miles the hour, to the cheerful clangour of their bells. These animals, when not addressed individually, are known by the generic name of "property" (*mâl*), though each has its own distinctive name,[3] and, for that matter, its peculiar temper

---

[3] The five mules of my first caravan were named Laili, Orange, Goldie, Brownie, and Blackie; four of the six mules

also. The bells rung by Quasimodo in Notre Dame (I had the book with me, a loan from Dr. Odling) are likened to *un bruyant attelage de mules espagnoles, piqué çà et là par les apostrophes du sagal;*[4] and a train of Persian mules in rapid motion is lively enough, as each animal lowers its head to its work and steps out with short quick paces, lifting bright hoof after hoof (the Persian shoe covers nearly all the foot), and making music wherever it goes, while the muleteers praise the foremost and chide those which lag. Night gradually settled down over the wild prospect. We talked of spirits that haunt the desert. Hafiz warns the traveller against the ghoul of the wilderness, that leads him astray by the mirage. "I was riding once," said my ghulam Sayyid, "with the Shadow of the Sultan across the desert between Isfahan and Yazd, by night. We saw an unknown fire in the darkness on our left. The prince bade me and another ride to it and

of my second were Sandal, Caprice (*názdár*), Ringlets (*Kákulí*), and Leader.

[4] This word *sagal* may perhaps be derived through the Moors from the Arabic *thaqqál*, meaning a carrier. The root is the same as the Hebrew *shekel*, which literally means a weight.

report. We galloped off, and galloped till morning, when the fire disappeared, and we had got never the nearer to it. We had lost our way, and regained the camp with difficulty in the evening." "Certainly," said Sayyid Ali, "there be evil spirits (*arwâh-i-khabís*). When I was in India, I lodged once in a house opposite to a graveyard. I was told that the spirits of the dead moved among the graves by night, with lights; but I did not believe such stories. One night I was coming home through the graveyard, when I saw a light hovering among the tombs. Had there been a man carrying it, I must have seen him; but there was no man, it was an evil spirit. I was so frightened that I do not remember how I got home." At this conjuncture, a flash appeared, or seemed to appear, for a moment, in the darkness before us. "That's a shot," said Zaki Beg; "I heard the report." I had heard nothing, and believed the flash to be simply fire struck by the heel of the leading mule. But a few minutes later, an indefinite black mass was seen to occupy the road; we closed up, marched on; and out of the darkness, with silent steps, came the gaunt figures of camels. It was a caravan carrying sugar and cloth from Yazd. We gave the men greeting, and passed by. They had heard our hoofs from afar, and had made a demonstration to show that they were armed and alert. Left alone with the desert, we steered our course towards a pyramidal mountain, a blot of deeper blackness on the dark horizon, assuming shape and sharper outlines as we drew nearer, till by midnight it was two miles on our left, and our guide bade us mark the cistern and shelter-house of Tabar. The ruins of the village stand at the foot of the hill; it succumbed in its struggle with the desert twenty years ago. Its resources were no greater than a spring of brackish water, and the tiny colony was unable to make head at once against isolation, drought, and the raids of Biluchis. This name we heard here for the first time; it is a word of fear to the people of these parts. The Biluchis, they say, come on their camels, thirty farsakhs in a night; they drink of this spring, and of other springs, salt and sweet, known to them among the mountains; and here, by the foot of this hill, they lie in wait for caravans, and do ravish the same when they get them into their net. Sleepiness is a sovereign balm against idle fears. We heard the dreadful words of our

Lost.

guide, and regarded them not, but looked on the shadowy mountain, as in a land of dreams, and rode on. We followed less the dim-descried road than a second and smaller peak which now arose as our landmark from afar. An hour's marching and fighting against sleep brought us under this beacon, an abrupt mass of rock rising over a river-bed (salt, of course) into which the road dips and disappears. At this interesting stage in the night's proceedings, our guide lost his way. We wandered up and down the river-bed for half an hour, then climbed the right bank, and entered a dolorous region of ridges, each directed towards the pole star, and leading nowhere. Dim sierras seemed to fence us round in the distance. Our guide, who had talked largely of his minute acquaintance with the road, which he had travelled twenty times (in his imagination), found no better counsel for us than to unpack and go to sleep, which we did. Sayyid Ali proposed tea and a qalyan; but I was asleep before these luxuries were ready. The night air was still and balmy; but the morning would have frozen water, had there been any to freeze. A few camel-thorn bushes afforded fuel for the servants and muleteers.

29th April, Fahraj, 7 farsakhs; 6 a.m. to 3 p.m.—By daylight we were astir, the guide cast about and recovered the road, and in an hour we reached the caravansarai of Chah-Kâvar. This stands near the bed of the river, with nothing but bare stony ridges and dry rocky hills all around; it is a large and well-built caravansarai, with a well of brackish water, but quite solitary and untenanted. A man and a child met us as we passed the door; they were migrating to Bâfk, and hoped to arrive there in the evening. The child walked all it could, and was carried the rest of the way on its father's back, with the few pounds of bread that were the sole provision of them both. We had now to cross the Dawiran range, and descend into the plain of Yazd. But Dawiran in these northerly regions sinks into a slender system of limestone hills, and the pass through which we came was only a break in the chain, traversable in an hour. Near the summit is an open abambar, with dirty but drinkable water. Here we breakfasted; then made our way between dry limestone peaks, and beheld a wonder, where we looked for none. Through a gap in the line of hills on our left, we became aware of a cloud-like whiteness hanging over a wide and hazy plain, with some indistinct shapes of blackness in the background. It was like the discovery of a new country, or a scene from fairy lands forlorn; so lofty seemed these phantom mountain-shapes, so cloud-like their snows, so remote seemed the plain, so far below us, with its paths and habitations of men, if it had any, all dissolved away and lost in the silvery mirage. Such was our first view of Shirkuh; I did not think then that I should reach the edge of those snows, and explore the recesses of the hills. Our present business was to reach Fahraj, distant now some fifteen miles, while Shirkuh was a good five-and-thirty miles on our left. To us looking across the sandy plain of Yazd, into which we were now decending, the mulberry-groves of Fahraj danced in the warm air, and seemed an island of verdure set in glassy summer seas. Four plodding hours carried us to that welcome shade. As we drew near to the village, I remembered those lines quoted by Lamb from Sir Philip Sidney's sonnet to sleep:—

> Take thou of me sweet pillow, sweetest bed,
> A chamber deaf to noise and blind to light,
> A rosy garland, and a weary head,—

and thought to myself, "Bed, pillow, and weariness I can guarantee; but I wonder what sort of mud quarters I shall get in place of that ideal chamber?" As it happened, however, Sayyid Ali's social accomplishments realized the whole thing to the letter. He fraternized at once with the owner of the first house to which we rode—a mullah of hospitable disposition and not uncultivated mind; I entered into a spacious court-yard shaded by mulberry trees, with a qanat stream behind it, and a good room at one side. The women cleared and swept the room, hoping that I should find it comfortable, and pointing out that the little things they left in the wall-niches (*táqchas*) would probably not be in my way. By this time the mules were unloaded, arrangements had been made for their feeding and ours; I unpacked my last small bottle of that dark Karman wine, drank it with satisfaction, shut the door, thereby excluding noise and light, and went to sleep without wreathing my head with the roses which the worthy mullah had placed on the table. It was almost sunset before I awoke and heard Sayyid Ali discoursing to the small boys of Fahraj, who had assembled to see his monster. "Yes," said he, "you shall see now,

Fahraj. 255

I will go in and wake him." I came out and caused an instantaneous dispersion of the assembly, but they came back and peeped round corners as long as there was any light. Their scrutiny, however, was not nearly so trying as that which I had lately endured in Bafk, where the women of the place ascended their housetops, and looked down on me from a rent in the domed roof of my chamber, whispering and giggling so persistently as to keep me in constant suspicion that my travel-worn garments must have given way in some unseen quarter.

Fahraj is beautifully shaded by mulberry trees, and its qanat, when we saw it, was full of cold snow-water from Shirkuh. The towers of Yazd, seventeen miles distant, can be seen from a slender minaret of mud, which I was inveigled into ascending, and speedily descended, finding that the frail structure could be contemplated with much greater peace of mind from below.

The distance between Bafk and Fahraj is eighteen farsakhs, but only some sixty miles. We marched it in thirty-one hours, including seven hours' halt at Khan-i-Panj, and four hours' enforced halt in the desert.

CHAPTER XII.

YAZD.

30TH APRIL TO 6TH MAY.

30th April, Yazd, 5 farsakhs; 11.30 a.m. to 4 p.m.
—After a fortnight's marching over waste places, from tiny village to village, where the eternal question is—Can we get straw and barley for the beasts, and bread for ourselves?—there hangs a glorious halo of expectancy over the day which shall fairly land one in a great city with a well-stocked bazaar, and in quarters more commodious than a peasant's hut, or the four bare walls of some mud fort. Sayyid Ali, in particular, had lofty hopes of our reception in Yazd. Before leaving Shiraz he had written a letter to the Hakimbashi or Court Physician of the Zill us Sultan in Isfahan, whom he knew already through the medium of the *Farhang* newspaper, edited by the Hakimbashi, and contributed to by Sayyid Ali, who wrote letters for

it from India upon things in general. The Hakimbashi replied by a letter to Karman, enclosing a firman from the Zill us Sultan for my honourable passage through his dominions, whereof Yazd is a part. We received this letter in Karman, to Sayyid Ali's great delight; and before leaving Fahraj, I despatched the ghulam Sayyid to show these credentials to the governor of Yazd, and apprise him of my coming. As we drew near Yazd, and entered the maze of sand-drifts which extend for two miles south of the city, Sayyid Ali's face assumed an expression of hope deferred, which was amusing enough. I did not care much, for my own part, whether the governor gave us quarters or left us to find them in a caravansarai. But as we drew near the suburbs, a crowd of horsemen broke upon us from behind the sand-hills on our left, and presently the miraculous apparition of a chariot descended from the sandy heights, and crossed our path. Sayyid Ali's face brightened. This was the expected *istiqbal* or escort of welcome. It was calculated to put one's modesty to the blush, my caravan was so humble, so travel-worn; I was riding the pony I had bought in Karman, a good little animal, but horribly out of condition; Sayyid

Ali was mounted on my old original grey horse of Shiraz, a beast remarkable for perpetual mange, and a fixed resolution not to fatten; while the bay Karman horse, having contracted a sore back, was led along triumphantly as a specimen of a walking skeleton. Zaki Beg enhanced the awe-inspiring grandeur of my train by the reverend aspect of his white steed, and the tattered antiquity of his garments. We were nevertheless received with immense deference. I took my seat in the carriage, and witnessed marvels of charioteering over watercourses and through the narrow bazaars of the city. We were conducted to the fort, where excellent quarters were assigned us in the Diwankhana or Government House. I had two large rooms, well carpeted, furnished with tables, chairs, and sofas, and looking out on a court-yard with trees and a tank of clear water. Tea and coffee were ready, and two huge trays of sweetmeats (for which Yazd is famed) were placed on the floor. Presently the Khan came to see me. He is the governor's brother, a slim youth with good features and an agreeable manner; the governor himself was absent in Isfahan. We became great friends during my stay in Yazd. Every morning and evening the

Khan came to see me, and we talked of all imaginable subjects over our tea and pipes. He was too young to care much about such serious topics as government or politics, but would listen with rapt attention to descriptions of the wonders of London, especially the Crystal Palace. His ignorance was sometimes amusing; for instance, when I showed him my maps, and pointed out Yazd, he was quite disappointed to see only a black spot instead of a bird's-eye photograph of the city of Yazd, which he had expected; and gravely suggested that I should have the map amended to suit his idea. On the third morning after my arrival, the Khan took me with him to a garden outside the city, where I saw Persian roses in full bloom along the banks of a watercourse lined with tiles and filled from a tank into which the water came tumbling over a little waterfall. We sat under the dome of the garden-house, and looked with pleasure at the pretty picture. This delight in gardens is an agreeable trait in the Persian character. A man will spend his money in making a garden that can never repay him, simply for the sake of having a place where he can sit in the mornings and evenings, smoke his qalyan and sip his tea, and enjoy the conversation of his friends beside a runnel of clear water, under the shade of trees, and within the sight and scent of flowers. Yet Persian flower-gardening is by no means adequate to the capabilities of the country. The principal flower is the rose, and it is little better than a dog-rose, though very sweet, and lovely to behold in its luxuriant plentifulness. A few days later, we spent a whole day in a larger garden at a greater distance from the city. The garden-house here is on a magnificent scale, but unfinished; the owner, late governor of Yazd, has been transferred to Khorasan, and his property in Yazd suffers from the absence of its master. A brick-lined tank, forty yards long by seven broad, occupies the centre of the garden. At the time of our visit, the rose-trees which border it were in full bloom, and two large bushes stood at its head, fragrant masses of white blossom. The pomegranate also was in flower. But the beauty of the garden was marred by a furious wind which arose in the evening, filling the air with dust, and overturning the tea-service which had been set beside the water. We were forced to retreat into an upper room and to shut the windows. The poor Khan, who was tormented with a grain of dust in his sole remaining eye (he had lost the other by accident while a boy), complained lamentably of this undesirable change. " The evening," said he, " ought to be the best time of the day in a garden, and now the evening has been spoiled. I had only one eye, and of course a grain of dust must get into it. This precious place, Yazd, is always full of wind and dust. They're catching it pretty hot in the city just now, I'll be bound." I consoled him as best I could, and gradually his eye grew better, the wind moderated, and we drove home in the dusk.

Speaking of the Khan, I ought to mention also his two big dogs. These are the progeny of a pair of mastiffs imported by the Zill us Sultan. They were nearly full-grown when I saw them, and seemed to me the largest dogs I had ever seen. No care having been taken with their education, they ran wild, fleeing from the approach of man. The Khan told me with pride that he had seen them pull down and kill a cow, an ass, and even a mule. Some day, I expect, they will pull down a man in open bazaar.

Yazd is a great trading mart. I saw many of its merchants, and found them intelligent, liberal, and anxious to hear about India and Indian trade. Haji Muhammád Taki, an old man of spare figure, and with that patriarchal cast of countenance which one sees sometimes in the East, told me with pride that he had lately given a bill of exchange on New York. He wished to know the cost of a railway from Yazd to Isfahan, and how much a luggage-train could carry. I estimated the cost for him at 5000*l.* a mile, and the freight of a train at 350 tons, or 2100 mule-loads. These figures filled him with dismay. He seemed to have been cherishing some faint sort of hope that a company of Yazd merchants, aided by the Government, might do something towards a railway to Isfahan. At the time of General Goldsmid's visit, ten years before, Haji Muhammad Taki had expressed similar hopes regarding the telegraph. Since then, the Government has made the telegraph, and the Yazd merchants use it much and value it highly; but the railway will probably be deferred for ever. The grand staple of Yazd is opium. All the fields round the city, while I was there, were white with poppy, and the time for gathering the opium had just begun. The poppy-heads are scored overnight by a comb with four or five short sharp teeth, and in the morning the exuded juice is removed with a spatula. The crop seemed a magnificent one;

I have not seen such tall strong poppy in India, with such full heads. One must also remark the growth of the trade during late years. The first hint I had of this was in Qazran, where the cultivation of poppy has been lately introduced, and is revenue-free. The Zarand district has recently begun to raise opium on loans advanced by Yazd merchants; thus, in Sar Asiab and Chatrut we were told that Gabrs from Yazd had come last year for this purpose, while in the neighbouring village of Gurchu the people had not yet learned poppy cultivation (*hanûz yâd na giriftand*). Kuhbanan seemed wholly given up to poppy. Though Isfahan is a greater centre of the opium trade than Yazd, yet as it was in Yazd that I got most of my information, I may as well record my statistics here, such as they are. The opium trade of Persia dates from the Chinese war. In the security afforded by the British occupation of Hong-Kong, Persian opium began to find its way to China. The prohibitive duties in the Indian ports were a great obstacle, and for a long time more opium went to Constantinople than to Hong-Kong. Then the route *viâ* Ceylon was struck out by certain merchants of Yazd, and now in these latter days opium is shipped direct for China from Bandar-Abbas by steamers of the Peiho Company. Last year's export was 6000 *peicul* or boxes; this year's export (1881) is expected to reach 8000 boxes. In 1871 the export was 4000 boxes. Thus the trade has doubled in ten years, and perhaps it is increasing now faster than ever before. Reduced to English figures,[1] the weight of 6000 boxes would be equivalent to 360 tons, and of 8000 boxes to 480 tons. These figures do not look formidable, especially when we remember that the Indian export is ten times as great. Still, if the Shah could but bring himself to spend some of his hoarded money on improving communications with the sea, it seems quite possible that the rivalry of Persian opium might be sensibly felt in India. The Persian price is somewhat lower than the Indian. Muhammad Taki Khan told me that the crude opium sold for 15 tomans the shahi man, and the finished

---

[1] One peicul = $10\frac{1}{2}$ shahi mans. The shahi man is 1280 misqals, each misqal being $\frac{3}{5}$ths of a tola; thus the shahi man = 512 tolas, and $10\frac{1}{2}$ shahi mans = $67\frac{1}{3}$ Government sers, or $134\frac{1}{2}$ lbs. Multiplying by 6000 we get 360 tons nearly. This corresponds pretty accurately with the result obtained by reckoning the peicul as equivalent to $1\frac{1}{4}$ cwt. English; more exactly, one paicool = $10\frac{1}{2}$ shahi mans, and $8\frac{1}{4}$ shahi mans = one hundredweight.

opium for 20 tomans. This would be as nearly as possible Rs. 10 and Rs. 13½ per ser; the Indian price for finished opium being Rs. 16. The Persian method of preparation is much more primitive, I fancy, than that practised in our opium factories. I watched the process in Isfahan; the opium was exposed on tiles to the heat of the sun, then kneaded vigorously, then exposed again, and so on; after the third or fourth kneading, it is made up into round flat-bottomed cakes of one pound each, and is ready for exportation. The colour is a clay yellow. Persian merchants are very eager to discover the process employed in India. As I have never seen the Ghazipur factory, I could not tell them, had I even been disposed to do so.

Next to opium, silk is a notable product of the Yazd district, but the industry has much declined of late. There were 1800 silk-houses here a few years ago, and there are scarce 150 now; so I was informed. The mulberry trees remain, overshadowing gardens and lanes with great luxuriance, and yielding a sweet white fruit, which is considered very wholesome as a corrective or preventive of the maladies incidental to the human frame in spring-time.

Yazd city has little that is worth seeing.

Caravansarais are numerous, but narrow and confined, with deep court-yards. The best is that of the Khan Wali, which is three-storied. The Khan's school, and the Musalla, are also buildings of some pretensions: the latter has a very deep court-yard, reached by a long descent of steps, at the bottom of which flows a watercourse full of blue mud deposited from the dyers' quarter. A foot of water flows over the mud, and the people wash in this stream and drink of it as if it were the cleanest imaginable. Perhaps the abambars are the chief glory of Yazd. Their domed roofs are really noble, and the wind-towers which surround them testify to the care taken to keep the water cool. The garrison of Yazd consists of 30 artillerymen and a regiment of infantry 400 strong. I saw the artillerymen and their guns—a six-pounder and a three-pounder of bronze, cast in Tabriz in the reign of Muhammad Shah. Situated in the heart of Persia, Yazd has no frontier tribes to keep in order, and its people, moreover, enjoy a reputation for peacefulness. The vice-governor told me that he had hardly any work to do, scarcely a dispute to settle; and I saw for myself the emptiness of his court-yard—strange contrast to the environs of an

Indian cutcherry. It is true that his brother had carried all the revenue work away with him to Isfahan; and perhaps the people might have no great confidence in the youth's capacity. I saw something of one case which had come before him; a man on the point of bankruptcy had made a personal visit to the house of a debtor of his, in the hope of recovering 600 tomans, and this visit had been represented to the vice-governor as an invasion of the privacy of the zanana, whereupon the unhappy bankrupt was seized and thrown into prison. Muhammad Taki interceded for him, and the vice-governor promised his release. The man's debts were 3000 tomans, part of which was due to Muhammad Taki himself. As for the prison, it was near my quarters; I saw the prisoners once or twice, in chains heavier than we use in India. They made their salaam, and seemed well enough nourished. Prosperity, indeed, is a notable feature of Yazd. Hardly a beggar was to be seen, and the busy bazaars and well-kept houses, as well as the dress of the people and the number of the merchants, were signs of a city supported by brisk trade. Every one with whom I spoke had something to say in praise of the Zill us Sultan, the Prince Governor of Isfahan, to whom Yazd is subject. When last year's scarcity threatened Yazd, he sent 2000 *kharwars* or ass-loads (about 580 tons) of wheat on his own mules to Yazd, to be stored as a first reserve. This restored confidence, and there was no further trouble. "We feel," said some of the men I spoke with, "that if a famine should come upon us, the Prince would not desert us, so we have confidence. He has suspended the revenue demand in the case of the poorer class of cultivators. He has given orders that they need not pay anything till this year's harvest has been got in." This year's harvest has been bountiful. We had ridden into Bafk under the evening sunlight between long fields of wheat and barley almost ready for the sickle ; and before I left Yazd barley harvest had begun. It was a pleasure to see such good crops. To return, however, to the Shahzada ; he abolished the export duty (*khurûj*) on opium, by which a former local governor of Yazd had succeeded in doing damage to the trade, and he is said to exact nothing from Yazd beyond the fixed revenue of the city. He has exerted himself to make the roads safe. The year before last, two highway robbers were caught near Karmanshahan, on the Karman road. The Prince was asked for orders, and telegraphed back, "Mortar them up," so they were encased in mortar, each at a gate of the city; I saw one of them. Nevertheless, the day of my arrival, Karmanshahan telegraphed that last night a caravan of tobacco and sugar from Yazd had again been plundered near the old place, two men killed, twelve wounded, and sixty camels driven off. The robbers were supposed to be Kashkais of Fars, who had come across the desert with a few days' provisions on their backs, and had lain in wait by that notorious *duzdgah* or robbers' haunt where low hills break the monotony of the desolate plain which extends from Sar-i-Yazd to Rafsinjan. Perhaps the recent change of government in Fars, of which more anon, had something to do with this daring raid.

The Gabrs or fire-worshippers of Yazd seem to deal chiefly in opium. They have a stone tower and platform, where they expose their dead, on a spur of a hill three miles south of Yazd. There are 150 families of Jews in Yazd engaged in the silk trade. They have fallen into great poverty, at least in externals. Their chief man called on me. He was wonderfully fair. He had a boon to solicit. It seems that a subscription was raised for the Jews of Yazd last year in Europe, and a sum of 400*l*. was forwarded to Teheran for them by Sir Moses Montefiore (such was the tale), but never got through the hands of the Teheran officials. Would I make inquiries in Teheran? I would not; but if the Jews would give me a written statement of their case, I had no objection to forward it to Sir Moses Montefiore, whom they regarded as their great patron. The man went away, and brought me a Hebrew letter two days later, which I forwarded, with a letter of my own, to a correspondent in London, who transmitted the papers to Sir Moses Montefiore's address, and in due time received a courteous reply to the effect that the petition of these poor Jews would be attended to. Although the man spoke with me quite in private, he made no complaint of oppression. He did complain of impoverishment in the famine, and of the Teheran officials who had stopped the expected remittance, on the strength of which the Jews had been borrowing from their Persian neighbours.

Yazd is out of the way of political information. The youthful vice-governor, being a native of Azarbaijan, regarded Russia as the greatest Power in the world. The merchants, like their class in all countries, took no interest in politics whatever.

CHAPTER XIII.

SHIRKUH.

6TH TO 11TH MAY: THIRTY-TWO FARSAKHS.

THE Khan had talked so much about Shirkuh and the wonders to be seen there, that I asked him for a ghulam, and planned a week's excursion in the mountains. He gave me not only a ghulam but also a *yuzbashi* or sergeant, a swell Turk, who had a fancy for a week's outing at other people's expense. I foresaw that this individual would be simply in the way, but being the Khan's guest, I could not dispute his good pleasure. Old Zaki Beg came with me, one servant, one muleteer, and two mules. We were a party of seven souls altogether, including a servant of my friend the Turk. Sayyid Ali stayed behind to entertain the Khan with his stories of India and the blessings of British rule.

6th May, Taft, 4 farsakhs; 9 a.m. to 2 p.m. —Our first march was to Taft, sixteen miles south-west of Yazd, and near the foot of Shirkuh. You cross the level stony plain, draw near to the hills, pass between two rocky knolls, and there is Yazd shut out from view behind you, while in front are the mulberry trees of Taft, a mass of foliage amidst which the houses can scarcely be discerned. The town fills a little plain or basin among low rocky hills, and its background is the mouth of a dark pass with cliffs two hundred feet high. A dry river-bed divides the plain; its water, taken off in the mountains, is led by a narrower channel down the main street of the town. A small covered bazaar, a gaily-painted Husainia, and some good houses, in one of which—the governor's—we found quarters; such are the modern glories of Taft. Holy men have lived here in time past. An old dome rises above the trees; it is empty, and the doors are gone, but the roof and walls still show beautiful work in blue and gold, with flowered tiles and fresco painting. Over the door, carved in wood, is the Arabic date, corresponding to the Christian year 1268. Hard by stand the ruins of the shrine built by Shah Niamat Ullah before he fixed his abode in Mahun. These are buildings of some extent, with the remains of handsome mural decorations. They are comparatively modern. Under the ancient dome are some beautiful tombstones of Yazd marble, pale yellow and white, carved with the graceful Arabic letter. The handsomest is quite plain but for the *kalima* or creed of Islam (there is no God but God, and Muhammad is the Prophet of God), cut in the polished yellow stone—a marvel of elegance. Another tombstone has the following inscription:—

DASHTAM SHAMA-I KI MIDIDAM BA NUR I O JAHÂN.
TUNDI I BAD I AJAL ÂMAD, RABUDASH NAGAHÂN.
TA ZI PESH I CHASHM I MA YEKDANA GOHAR DUR SHUD,
DIDA I GHAMM DIDA-AM SHUD RUZ O SHAB GOHARFISHÂN.
AZ FIGHÂNAM MURGH O MAHI GAR BINALAD, DUR NIST;
NÂLA I MAN SANGRA HAR LAHZA ÂRAD DAR FIGHÂN.
SAL I UMRASH YAZDIH, DAR HAFTA I MAH I RAJAB,
SHUD BAR FIRDAUS I BARRIN ABDUL ALI NAU JAWAN.
HASHT SAD O CHIHIL BUD O HASHT AZ HIJRA I KHAIR UL BASHAR. . . . .

Which might be rendered freely thus:—

"I had a light that lighted all the world for me. Fate, like a violent wind, whirled it away. Since my unique pearl vanished from my sight, my sad eyes, by night and day, have teemed with pearls, called tears. Marvel not if bird and fish wail at the sound of my mourning, for the very rocks have learned continually to re-echo my grief. In his eleventh year, on the seventh of the month Rajab, young Abdul Ali passed to Paradise on high. It was eight hundred and forty and eight from the glad tidings of the Flight. . . . ."

The rest is wanting. The date would be 1477 A.D. It seemed to me that this expression of a father's grief for the death of his son was worth transcribing as a touch of nature transmitted across four centuries from the distant East.

In the evening I ascended the hill to the south of Taft, and visited a natural well in a cleft of the rock, which of course is reputed to be of unfathomable depth. Taft looked extremely pretty, with its old fòrt on a rocky knoll rising out of the sea of foliage, and its white poppy-fields fringing all the outskirts. The song of nightingales came up from the mulberry groves. I sat half an hour, enjoying the view, and talking to the men who were with me. Thence we went to the house of one of the local notables, whom we found drinking tea with his friends in a court-yard overshadowed by vines, and crossed by a qanat-stream flowing through a little tank. I sat down and had tea and a qalyan. The people were a little shy at first, but soon became talkative and friendly. Why did I not allow my rice to be cooked with oil? was there any religious prohibition? Thus is the traveller continually reminded of the ceremonial law which lies like an incubus on Islamitic countries, binding men from the cradle to the grave, and prompting them to recognize a system of similar tyranny in every habit which caprice or convenience may recommend to the European stranger. I do not know whether I succeeded in making these worthy people believe that the reason of my abstinence was simply a natural dislike of greasy dishes. It was more difficult to explain the difference between the Protestant religion and the Armenian. From theology we passed to geography. I was catechized by a learned doctor as to the number of zones (*aqlîm*). After some misunderstanding, we came together on the ecliptic, of which the doctor had a perfectly correct idea. I explained to him that our torrid zone extended between the extreme northern and southern points on the line of the ecliptic; and he explained to me that *his* zones were reckoned from the equator to the poles, according to each half-hour's difference in the length of the day; also that the space of twelve degrees on each side of the equator is uninhabited. He then began to ask about Europe, and lamented the death of the Emperor of Russia, whom he called the Imperator i Aazam, or Most Great Emperor, the autocrat of all Europe, in his eyes.

After dinner, the governor came in with a musician, and also with some good red wine. We had some odes of Hafiz sung in a style perhaps two degrees better than the usual bellowing. The governor was highly sensible of the charms of poetry. He looked at me and shook his head mournfully when the singer lamented the want of good faith in these latter days (*in zamân wafâ na darad*); the fact is that he had the governorship of Miankuh and Pusht-i-kuh last year, as well as Taft, but some rival had carried off the two former at the end of the year. What struck me most, however, was the ejaculation *Amân, amân! nishan i kaaba kujast? ki bimurdim dar dashtash*—"Mercy, mercy! where is the sign of the kaaba? for we are perishing in the desert, seeking it." It was not only that the words recalled long marches when the halting-place delayed to come into view hour after hour; but they are, after all, the cry of failing faith in all countries and times, and the doubts of Hafiz might be rendered in the most modern of English words—

> And long the way appears, that seemed so short
> To the unpractised eye of sanguine youth;
> And high the mountain-tops, in cloudy air,
> The mountain-tops where is the throne of Truth,
> Tops in life's morning sun so bright and bare!

7th May, Deh Bala, 4 farsakhs; 7.30 a.m. to 1 p.m.—So much for Taft. We marched next day up the bed of the river, between walls of rock which gradually closed in on us, till we had precipices 250 feet high on either hand. An isolated tower of rock was pointed out as the fort of one Badi, a *pahlwân* or mighty man of valour in those parts. He seems to have been an historical personage, and to have been hunted down and killed near the old fort of Taft. Our guide looked with pride on the precipices, and called my attention to their impregnability. The young men of Taft had unfortunately shared his sentiments four years ago, and had created some disturbance, for which they were killed, imprisoned, or transported to the Garmsir between the Shiraz mountains and the Persian Gulf. I could get no correct account of this little rebellion, which seems to have been suppressed with vigour.

Taft, however, has suffered more from famine than from the sword. At a census taken fourteen years ago, its population was 11,745; a second census six years ago showed only 3353. The famine of 1869-70 had come between. The present population of the place is about 5000.

I had been told of a wonderful waterfall at the head of this ravine, 180 *gaz* in height, or about 500 feet. As we ascended the ravine, the Taft watercourse merged in a natural stream flowing pleasantly over stones and among boulders. Turning into a fork which branched off to the right, we passed above a solitary house built on a ledge level with the stream, while the banks on either hand, for a quarter of a mile, were cut into little terraces of rice and wheat, and lined with walnut, mulberry, and sinjad trees, and with wild pomegranate and coriander bushes. It was a pretty sight. Scrambling over the rocks, we reached the head of the ravine, and found a slender stream of water falling thirty feet into a basin, and thence ninety feet to the bottom. This was the famous waterfall. In a hollow of the rock, some forty feet above the bed of the ravine, a picnic party were drinking tea and cooking soup. I climbed up, and had some tea and a smoke, but could not wait for breakfast. I had my own breakfast farther on, under a rock beside the stream. Our way led us up the left-hand branch of the main ravine, by a gradual ascent, to a plateau of level rock, where, nevertheless, a small village-fort contrives to subsist on the produce of a few fields. We were now on a shoulder of Shirkuh, and a few miles more carried us into the heart of the mountain, where Deh Bala stretches up a long ravine that rises ever more steeply to the topmost snow-covered ridge. Unlike the passes through which we had been travelling all day, this ravine is nowise black and empty, but bright with terrace-fields on either side of a full sparkling stream, and overshadowed by all manner of goodly fruit-trees, in new leaf of the freshest, loveliest green. For six miles our road lay among scenes like this, under the shadow of apple, pear, and quince trees, white and red with blossom, of broad-leaved fragrant walnut trees, stately planes, and the lavish foliage of mulberries. The river, now on this side now on that, threw its clear snow-water over the rocks, or into bright shingly pools; while innumerable channels, taken off at higher points, after irrigating the terraced wheat and poppy, came pouring out in crystal showers through the stone walls which fenced the upper margin of the road. Behind the leafy screen great rock-walls rose, dark and impracticable; while before us the gorge narrowed and closed against the huge snow-crowned rampart of Shirkuh ridge itself, suspended highest of all, like a white cloud in the blue air. We found quarters in the house of a Haji, close by the river. The first thing I did on arriving was to go and bathe in a pool. The water was delightfully cold. A pile of granite boulders above the terrace-fields gave me a fine view of the long straggling village and the cliffs that shut it in and hold up the snow-covered summits of the mountain. I wished to cross Shirkuh by the head of this ravine, but everybody agreed that the road was blocked with snow, and I did not like to risk the mules.

8th May, Manshar, 4 farsakhs; 8 a.m. to 1 p.m.—Accordingly, next day we marched to Manshar, descending the ravine and turning sharp to our right, passing on our way two little villages, and the large village of Tizarjan, the best of all those which Shirkuh hides in its well-watered recesses. Tizarjan has a river somewhat smaller than that of Deh Bala, but a much wider area of field and wood, filling a broad hollow at the foot of the highest peak of Shirkuh—a noble mountain capped with a crown of rock many hundred feet high. A broad band of snow lay at the foot of the crown, and its summit was deep in snow. The snow would disappear towards the end of summer, but in clefts and hollows of the rock (so I was assured) the accumulations of countless winters are stored up, safe from the sun. Passing this lovely valley with regret, we turned aside to Manshar, and found that it too lay in a hollow, less broad than that of Tizarjan, and watered by two small streams. It is the largest village of Shirkuh, has a mosque, and a few shops. Here again a Haji's house received us; the old man took so much trouble on my account that I was quite ashamed. I picked up a guide here, who proved rather an amusing fellow. He came with me for a walk in the afternoon, up a hill-side where the gleam of water flowing over a shelving rock had caught my eye. I found the place lined with grass, through which the little streamlet made its way, and half-way up the hill was a small plateau planted with pollard willows, with a pool in the middle where the streamlet was dammed. They call a dam *istakh* or *salkh*, a strange word, seemingly old Persian. My guide was very anxious that I should bath in the pool, which possessed medicinal virtues, and was resorted to by patients from Yazd; but I had bathed sufficiently in the river below. He then began to discourse freely about local affairs, complained of oppression, and said the kalantar would take ten tomans as his *mudakhil* or perquisite in consequence of my visit. This smote upon my conscience, but there was no remedy, and probably the sum was exaggerated. "The people," said my companion, "desire to be under your banner" (*zir i alam i shumá*), i.e., under British rule—had they only a definite notion of England as distinguished from Farangistan generally. Then he proceeded to glorify the mineral products of Shirkuh. "Under the snows," he said, "are crystals (*durr* or *qalam*) as long as one's finger, which grow there like mushrooms." He himself had watched one grow. A boxful of them was collected and sent to Farangistan a few years ago. As for the village people, they are Bâbîs,[1]

---

[1] The Bâb or Gate was a native of Nirez who preached a communistic and mystical religion that had much in it to

and have community of wives and daughters (*zan o dukhtar i hamdigar hilál midánand*); of which custom my companion advised me to take advantage, as a remedy against loneliness during the rest of my stay in Manshar. I hastened to turn the conversation to less questionable subjects. We sat and looked over the valley bathed in the quiet evening light. A cuckoo was calling as we descended the hill towards the groves and broad vine-trellises of Manshar. We crossed a swift brook flowing from the snows that rose against the sky on our right. I thought I had never looked upon a prettier scene. In the Haji's garden of apple, plum, and apricot trees, I enjoyed a qalyan and tea before dinner. I slept in an upper room overlooking the garden, and was wakened twice in the night by the rapturous singing of nightingales, whose wild music burdened every bough.

9th May, Sakhvid, 5 farsakhs; 8 a.m. to 3 p.m.—Next day we marched across Shirkuh by the Manshar pass, a low saddle-back, just reaching to the level of the snow at this time of year. The country on the southern side of

attract the free-thinking Persian mind. He was put to death in 1850.

the mountains is utterly unlike the valleys and ravines which nestle in their bosom on the side next Yazd. When we reached the crest of the pass, we saw a long bare slope, of the kind so familiar to the traveller in central Persia, extending downwards till it sank into a desert plain broken here and there by hills, "mere ugly heights and heaps," which rose into jagged ridges in the eastern or left-hand part, and subsided into mere undulations towards the right. The top of the slope, as distinguished from the actual mountain-side above it, lay considerably higher than the valleys on the Yazd side; in fact, for all their southerly aspect, the walnut trees in the gardens of Nid and Sakhvid were only beginning to come into leaf. While the rest of the caravan descended the mountain-side and marched round a spur, I went with my guide by a mountain path which led us up a rocky peak, and thence down a ravine, where a snow-fed brook tumbled among rocks and grass. Coming down upon the road, we walked on, thinking the mules in advance, but in half an hour we heard a shot, and saw them two miles behind. We sat beside a water-channel and awaited their coming. A plane-tree gave us shade, and bushes of sweet briar perfumed the air all along the banks. When the mules came up, we marched along the slope as far as Nid, where, finding no quarters, we went on to Sakhvid, four miles further, and got good rooms in the Zabit's house. These villages at the back of the mountains have no such charms as Deh Bala and Manshar. They stand on the bare slope, overlooking the desert, and are watered by rivers or brooks much smaller than those which have scooped out the ravines on the northern side. One consequence of their exposed situation is a comparative deficiency of trees. In the evening I went up a hill above Sakhvid, and surveyed the villages which dotted the narrow strip of qanat-irrigated land between the foot of the slope and the desert. These, with the villages on the slope, make up the Pusht-i-kuh district. One of them, by name Irnan, is distinguished by a quaint rocky hill which rises above it, some 800 feet high, scarped all round, and accessible (I was told) by one path only, and that not practicable for everybody. The hill is quite isolated, but does not seem to have been fortified, probably because it is waterless above, though there are some slender springs at its base. As we rode past on the long slope, and looked at the village below us and fifteen miles distant, one of the party told a story of a yuzbashi of Karman, who, taking disgust at Government service, started with five companions to plunder Irnan, and succeeded in gaining possession of the fort, but was ultimately exterminated with his followers by soldiers from Yazd. This happened four or five years ago. The exploit was spoken of in that tone of moral indifference which distinguishes Persian criticism of banditti; indeed, the yuzbashi was rather lamented as a loss to the country, being a man (they said) of a dauntless and desperate courage, who regarded the life of a man no more than that of a dog.

10th May, Mirza Hashim's hamlet, 4 farsakhs.—From Sakhvid we had to retrace our steps to the Manshar Pass. Wishing to make an easy march, I determined to halt on this side of the pass, in whatever hamlet we could find. We stayed by the way in Nid, to get wheat for the cattle and bread for ourselves. Here I had a second experience of the inconveniences attending *sursât*. The kalantar came to me privately and said we had taken stores to the value of fourteen krans; which I paid him. The Khan who accompanied me got news of this, and promptly turned back and enforced repayment of the money. Thence we marched along the slope, looking down upon the hazy plain, with its white patches of kavir and its dark patches that mark villages, situated mostly at the edge of the salt, where the subterranean drainage from the mountains rises to the surface. We halted at a hamlet called after one Mirza Hâshim, where we found only women. A respectable old lady placed her house at our disposal, and, with her handmaidens, waited on us diligently. I went out in search of a bathing-place, and discovered a spout in a ravine, under which I sat; the snow-water seemed to cut one in two. In the afternoon I went with my guide up a hill crowned with huge blocks of grey granite, piled on each other and weather-worn into hollow shapes—a common feature in the skirts of Shirkuh. A smart shower drove us into the crevices for refuge, and afterwards the setting sun lighted up the desert with great distinctness, and showed us the snowy tops of the mountains of Baonât in Fars, nearly a hundred miles to the south-west. I had picked up some information concerning the routes across the intervening desert, which here is encroached upon by no such fringe of villages as below Sakhvid; we could see only bare stony plain, with ridges and hillocks here and there, and the thin white line of kavir threading it from left to right. The Prophet of Thieves in Lar had told me that the desert and kavir between Fars and Karman was the salvation of the latter province, which else had lain quite at the mercy of the bold spirits of Fars. Nevertheless, the desert is crossed by caravans bringing wheat from Baonât, and also, as in the recent affair at Karmanshahan, by bands of thieves. My guide called my attention from topographical inquiry to his own private affairs. He had for years followed the fortunes of a dervish, who conversed with animals. "I have myself seen him," said the ex-disciple, "engaged in conversation with every species of animal" (*suhbat bâ hama jur jânwarân*). When the time of the dervish's dissolution approached, he went with his disciple into the desert, sat down in a suitable place for dying, and bade his pupil gather a stone and a certain herb, and carry them for tokens to a village which he indicated. The man did so, and the elders of the village produced a shroud, and went in search of the dervish; found him dead, shrouded him duly, and buried him in their village with honour. The unfortunate disciple might have emulated his master, but a woman got hold of him, as he said (*gír-i zan shudam*), and made him the father of seven children, whom he was unable to support. All this he narrated pensively to me as he sat on the top of the rock, holding his long gun across his knees; presently he began to weep, and desired to enter my service. This being impossible, we returned to the hamlet, where I slept outside for fear of the insect tribe.

11*th May, Mahriz, 5 farsakhs; 6.30 a.m. to 1 p.m.*—The back of Shirkuh looked cold and frosty next morning, with its thousand feet of dark precipice capped with snow. My guide offered to take me to the top by an easy road. " You wouldn't know you were ascending," he said, " and from the top you would see all the world." But we had no time for such excursions. Re-crossing the saddle-back, and leaving Manshar on our left, we marched down a ravine as long as that of Deh Bala, but narrower, and filled with a larger river. Between the river and the cliffs, for the distance of six miles till the ravine falls too steeply for cultivation, straggles the village of Gosha. We rode rejoicing under leafy shade, through stone-fenced lanes, past houses whose wooden gables and galleries recalled the traditional Swiss châlet. But such happiness can never last long in Persia. After an hour and a half the dark cliff-walls closed in and took the river to themselves, while our road turned off to the right. All at once we seemed to leave the mountains behind us with their greenery, and to be condemned to brown, barren plains once more. The hill-side we descended was a slope of rock, and the julgah or dry stony strath between Shirkuh and the Bohrak range lay at its feet, showing two little villages which tap the Gosha river ere it has well sunk into the shingle. Over this dreary julgah we marched ten miles, having Shirkuh on the right, and the unprofitable ridge of Bohrak on the left. Shirkuh presented some noble views, though empty of human habitation. Under its south-eastern peak, perhaps the highest and snowiest of all, there is no village nor room for a village; all is rock and ravine and precipice. Farther on, a cleft called the Dark Pass (*Tang-i-tarik*) pierces the mountain. Some parts of the Gosha ravine, indeed, had almost deserved that name, where we drew rein to admire the height and steepness of the cliffs, and the contrast of their sullen blackness with the brightness and life below. At a small shelter-house with an abambar we met a party of travellers breakfasting, and shared their bread and curds. At length Mahriz disclosed itself behind a low ridge of rocks. It occupies a plateau at the foot of Shirkuh, much like Taft, but somewhat higher and nearer the mountains. A space of two miles square is covered with mulberry trees, among which Mahriz lies hidden away. We went to the Zabit's house, and found him out, but he came back in hot haste before evening, from a village three farsakhs distant, where he had been collecting revenue. We talked together for some time before dinner. I slept on a Persian four-post bedstead, a gigantic structure, upon the roof, under magnificent moonlight, and in full view of Shirkuh, its blackness and its snows. I had never seen anything so romantic; it was the "mondbeglänzte zaubernacht" in an Eastern land, where the topographical surveyor has still left some room for the imagination. Waking in the night, I seemed to be floating away through the wonderful prospect.

12th May, Yazd, 6 farsakhs.—Next day we returned to Yazd. In Muhammadabad we halted to avoid the heat of the day. Our quarters were a garden-house; I had the whole upper storey to myself, and the gardener brought me mulberries. Some merchants' sons picnicking here came to see me; the father of one of them was in business in Baku. These young fellows seemed to be leading an indolent, easy life. As the weather grew hotter they would move on to Taft and the cool valleys of Shirkuh, where their fathers owned summer-houses. A great part of the Shirkuh villages thus belongs to merchants of Yazd. Some country bumpkins also came upstairs to see the stranger. I invited them to sit down, and discovered from them something about the revenue system of the village. Late in the afternoon we marched on to Yazd. The evening sun was shining behind us as we drew near to the city, lighting up the plain and the black mountain-masses behind it and on either side. The air was fresh and clear after the rain of two days before. I turned in my saddle and looked with gladness over the wide view—the golden-brown plain, the golden-green crops, the dark mountains, and the trees and wind-towers of distant villages. The road was full of Yazd women riding away from the city on mules and asses, with servants male and female walking or riding after. My Yazd ghulam (the ghulam Sayyid had been sent back to Karman after my arrival in Yazd, with a letter of satisfaction) undertook to explain this female emigration. "They are going to eat mulberries," he said. "Married women fall sick of some mysterious ailment in the spring, and say to their husbands, 'My dear, I know I shall never be better till I have gone into the country to eat mulberries. In such and such a village my mother's sister-in-law's son owns a garden, and I am sure he will put me up for a few days;' and the man is not her mother's sister-in-law's son at all, but some young fellow she knows. So the husband consents, and at the end of a few weeks his wife comes back to him, looking fresh and cheerful, having recovered her good looks, which she was afraid of losing;" and the old rascal grinned wickedly as he looked at the veiled figures riding by. As we entered the gates of Yazd, a cavalcade came to meet us, headed by Sayyid Ali, clean-shaved and in high spirits. The Khan came to see me at once, and said he had felt quite lonely since

I left. An excellent dinner was waiting for me, and it was with satisfaction that I drank my wine and iced sherbet, and reflected on my excursion to Shirkuh. Next day was given to writing letters, and in the evening we packed our baggage once more for the road. The Khan gave me the ghulam who had accompanied me to Shirkuh, and also a Shatir-bashi or kind of Commandant of the body-guard, a handsome and well-built young Turk, *fruges consumere natus*, who I foresaw would be a mere burden; but there was nothing for it but to accept him with a good grace. He wanted to go to Isfahan, and thought this a good opportunity of doing so at the expense of other people, *i.e.*, of the villagers from whom he was empowered to levy *sursât*.

END OF VOL. I.

www.ingramcontent.com/pod-product-compliance
Lightning Source LLC
Chambersburg PA
CBHW030820230426
43667CB00008B/1306